More Praise for *The Gamification Revolution*

"Zichermann and Linder pull together the most interesting case studies, important models, and critical conclusions about gamification into a single book that is a must-read for any strategic, marketing, or HR executive."

—KEN FAVARO, Senior Partner, Booz & Company

"In today's fast-paced world, people are more distracted than ever. To stand out, you'll need to cut through the noise and get them engaged. *The Gamification Revolution* will teach you the essential building blocks for achieving long-term success and growth."

—JESSE REDNISS, Senior VP, NBCU

"Gabe is a key thought leader and industry proponent for Gamification. *The Gamification Revolution* highlights best practices for the use of game mechanics in business contexts. This is an important framework that all major organizations will eventually need to leverage as they evolve their business models as well as relationships with clients and partners."

—TIM CHANG, Partner, Mayfield Fund, and Forbes Midas
List Inductee

"Finding ways to proactively change tack to keep a competitive edge can be difficult in an increasingly dynamic business environment. *The Gamification Revolution* presents exciting concepts to help managers increase engagement and make their business as dynamic as the environment in which it competes."

—DAN BALLARD, Director of Revenue Management,
Clear Channel Outdoor

"Gamification is at the confluence of Sales 2.0 and Social Selling and is not understood by sales leaders. Zichermann and Linder propose a pragmatic approach to gamification that will provide breakthrough results. Sales is the last bastion of corporate innovation, and this spectacular read is a must for any sales leader."

—HI LEVA, Senior VP of Sales Operations, Clear Channel Outdoor

THE
GAMIFICATION
REVOLUTION

HOW LEADERS LEVERAGE
GAME MECHANICS
TO CRUSH THE COMPETITION

GABE ZICHERMANN
JOSELIN LINDER

Mc
Graw
Hill
Education

New York Chicago San Francisco Lisbon London Madrid Mexico City
Milan New Delhi San Juan Seoul Singapore Sydney Toronto

1 2 3 4 5 6 7 8 9 0 QFR/QFR 1 9 8 7 6 5 4 3

ISBN 978-0-07-180831-6
MHID 0-07-180831-0

e-ISBN 978-0-07-180832-3
e-MHID 0-07-180832-9

Library of Congress Cataloging-in-Publication Data

Zichermann, Gabe.
    The gamification revolution : how leaders leverage game mechanics to crush the competition / by Gabe Zichermann and Joselin Linder.
        pages cm
    ISBN 978-0-07-180831-6 (alk. paper) — ISBN 0-07-180831-0 (alk. paper)
    1. Social media—Marketing. 2. Internet games—Psychological aspects. 3. Customer loyalty. I. Linder, Joselin. II. Title.
    HF5414.Z53 2013
    658.4'012—dc23

                                                                    2013002280

McGraw-Hill books are available at special quantity discounts to use as premiums and sales promotions or for use in corporate training programs. To contact a representative, please e-mail us at bulksales@mcgraw-hill.com.

This book is printed on acid-free paper.

To Zachary, Addison, Billy, Julia, and Gabriel—
our favorite game-playing millennials

CONTENTS

CONNECTING, ENGAGING, AND LEVERAGING YOUR CUSTOMER BASE

ACKNOWLEDGMENTS

GABE ZICHERMANN I would like to thank my family and friends, with special props to Gary Henkle, Ivan Kuo, and Taavi Lindmaa, for their help with research and interviews for this book.

Most important, however, credit for this book project goes to the gamification community. Your endless support—at GSummit and GSummitX Meetups, in online discussions and in random street-side encounters—provides the emotional fuel for this endeavor.

Every time a company, nonprofit, or government agency changes behavior using gamification, I get a little giddy. That's because it's predicated on something extraordinarily powerful: your optimistic belief that the world can be improved through better design. This view makes me dream of brighter futures, and I hope this book's presentation of gamification as a core business strategy honors your faith and trust—both in our important movement and the work we do together.

Thank you.

JOSELIN LINDER I would like to thank Neil Moss, Bill Burton, Shoshi Derrow, Jamie McDonald, Danny Peter, Dan Ballard, and others who read through early drafts of the manuscript and offered invaluable advice. I also want to thank Jacquie Flynn and Joelle Delbourgo for their ongoing support and—as always—excellent book title suggestions.

I want to also extend my appreciation to everyone at Dopamine and Gamification.Co, especially Taavi Lindmaa, for their hours of help, input, and explanation.

To my family: I couldn't do anything without you. And to Aaron: Thank you for everything all the time. I love you.

GO DEEPER WITH THE GAMIFICATION REVOLUTION APP

In order to make ideas from *The Gamification Revolution* easier to put into practice, we've developed an app that you can access at http://gamrev.com. The app, which works on all smartphones and computers, lets you take optimized notes, go much deeper into this fascinating subject, and easily share relevant information with colleagues and friends. The app includes these tools:

➤ *Dozens of videos.* These videos include numerous exclusives from leading experts on how to create and sustain engagement with employees and customers, and they can be unlocked as you progress through the book.

➤ *Social reading and collaboration.* Invite colleagues or friends to read with you, easily take and share notes and ideas with the community, discuss the book, and drive change within your organization quickly and easily.

➤ *Social media lists.* These lists include direct Twitter links to the key people and companies profiled in the book so you can easily engage with the experts.

➤ *Important links.* Beyond Twitter, we've included links to enable you to further research the companies profiled in the book and more.

And, of course, it wouldn't be an app about gamification unless it was fun and a little bit challenging. Visit http://gamrev.com today and start accelerating your organization's engagement strategy now.

INTRODUCTION

Theodore Roosevelt once said, "When you play, play hard; when you work, don't play at all."

It probably comes as no surprise that Teddy Roosevelt believed in a tough work ethic. He was a strict task master despite his image as an outgoing, jovial man for whom they named the teddy bear. In fact, he himself was an overachiever who went from meek asthmatic to Nobel Prize winner. His legacy as one of the most highly regarded U.S. presidents is rarely challenged.

The idea that work and play cannot coexist is still a widely accepted truth. Throughout many of our own childhoods, we were taught the rules about when we could unbutton our metaphoric top buttons. The line between work and play was plain. It was defined, and it was very, very serious.

However, this is simply no longer true.

As a result of a series of changes in demographics, technology, and the competitive landscape, smart companies, as well as nonprofits and governments, are increasingly turning to play and games as a way of radically reinventing their organizations. They are engaging customers as never before, aligning employees, and driving innovation that seemed virtually impossible only a decade ago. They've realized that their strength is in marshaling

FIGURE I.1 *Gamification* is the process of engaging audiences by leveraging the best of loyalty programs, game design, and behavioral economics.

the intelligence, motivation, and—most critically—**engagement** of their communities to drive their business objectives.

This concept is called *gamification*—that is, implementing design concepts from games, loyalty programs, and behavioral economics to drive user engagement (Figure I.1). This idea has been percolating beneath the surface of modern business for years, but it is finally coming into its own. Gartner Group predicts that by 2015, nearly 70 percent of the world's largest enterprises will be using it, driving 50 percent of all innovation. Moreover, M2 Research expects that U.S. companies alone will be spending $3 billion per year on gamification technologies and services before the end of the decade. These stats become even more impressive once you realize that the term "gamification" doesn't even appear ranked in Google Trends until 2010.

The runaway success of gamification—as this book will show—belies a core concept that is missing from nearly every other business strategy book of the last half-century:

Without employee and customer **engagement**, the best laid strategies and tactics are **doomed to fail**.

Consider the example of FoxMeyer Drugs. In 1993, the company was the fourth largest drug distributor in the United States. The company began a project with the software management firm SAP and the business management consulting firm Andersen Consulting (now Accenture) for the purpose of transitioning to a new enterprise resource plan (ERP), which would serve as a back-end system for the automation of their warehouses. Despite an aggressive 18-month rollout program, the company did one major thing wrong: it forgot to engage the staff.

Thousands of workers looked on in horror as the company began shuttering multiple warehouses in anticipation of the increased efficiency promised by the new software. Entirely disengaged from management at any meaningful level, employees didn't know what else to think but that they were being replaced by machines. While their fears weren't entirely unfounded, at that time it wasn't actually the company's plan to lay off most of the employees, but the executives didn't pass their thinking along to the employees. This lack of clarity, information, or direction from the company's leadership team was a disaster in the making.

Rather than stand idly by and watch, a group of employees staged an attack, sabotaging both the new software system as well as the facility itself. Once the software had finally been implemented over the active resistance of the employees, it failed to meet expectations. What might otherwise have been a smooth transition proved an utter catastrophe—destroying morale and profoundly impacting the future of FoxMeyer. By 1998, the $5 billion company was bankrupt.

Although FoxMeyer, Andersen, and SAP have traded accusations in court for years over improprieties in the way this ERP transition was handled, there was no mistaking that the lack of engagement between management and its employee base was critical to the demise of both the new processes and the company itself.

But the truth is, we don't have to look for so dramatic an example to see the peril in a lack of engagement between not only management and employees but also between management, employees, *and* business strategies. If your organization is like most, your IT department's history is probably littered with dozens of failed projects that died because employees rejected them. In fact, the Standish Group's 2011 CHAOS report estimates that 21 percent of all enterprise software projects fail—with costs running into the billions—often because of lack of use and engagement.

On the customer side, the stories are even more dramatic. According to Microsoft Research fellow Chao Liu, the average new visitor to a website will decide whether or not to stay there in *10 seconds or less.* And if they make it past 30 seconds, you are lucky to get two whole minutes of their attention. On the mobile platform, engagement is even more grim: according to mobile information experts Localytics, over 69 percent of mobile app users access an app a total of 10 times or less. Research from Flurry analytics further shows that only 25 percent of users come back to a given app in a 90-day period (Figure I.2).

The enormity of that dropoff in engagement isn't lost on app developers whose focus is primarily on smartphone users. And interestingly enough, a decline in the average attention span isn't just happening to them. Customers at their desks, driving to malls, and even sitting in front of televisions are getting harder and harder to attract to your brand.

As a business, your success depends on getting and keeping the attention of both your customers and your employees. Unfortunately, getting that attention in the first place is becoming increasingly more difficult to accomplish. A 2011 study revealed that four-year-olds who were subjected to fast-paced cartoons over nine-minute intervals had markedly worse executive functioning skills than those who weren't. Tracey Marks, MD, a leading psychiatrist with a focus on mind-body connection, believes adults may not lose executive function in the same way children do, but this is largely

Loyalty by Application Category

Category	30 Day Retention	60 Day Retention	90 Day Retention	Frequency of Use/Week
News	74%	57%	43%	11.0
Medical	72%	55%	43%	3.0
Reference	70%	55%	42%	10.7
Productivity	72%	38%	35%	6.0
Navigation	73%	33%	30%	6.0
Health & Fitness	65%	35%	30%	7.0
Education	72%	34%	30%	4.0
Weather	74%	38%	27%	10.5
Business	71%	33%	26%	5.0
Music	65%	32%	26%	5.0
Finance	71%	33%	21%	6.0
Sports	73%	30%	20%	4.0
Travel	61%	25%	17%	7.0
Utilities	55%	19%	16%	7.7
Games	72%	23%	14%	7.4
Social Networking	61%	19%	12%	6.0
Entertainment	51%	15%	12%	2.6
Books	72%	23%	12%	10.0
Lifestyle	50%	8%	5%	8.0
Average	67%	32%	25%	6.7

FIGURE I.2 This Flurry analytics chart, Loyalty by Application, shows the numbers of users who return to particular applications regularly.

due to their ability to filter out much of the noise. In other words, all of our filtering of the competing ideas, websites, and projects appearing on our computers, televisions, and mobile devices in our offices and homes, and even during our car rides home, is actually keeping us from connecting with much of what we see. It is increasing our stress and potentially making us dumber. The trend isn't slowing down, and it is affecting industries across the spectrum— from the civil service to finance, engineering to retail.

But there is one industry that seems to be immune to the shattering of focus: games. While from the outside, games might seem like part of the problem, they are in fact the one place where we are increasingly finding ourselves both connecting and *enjoying* our connection.

In fact, year after year consumers spend an increasing amount of time playing games. From 2002 to 2012, the Census Bureau estimated that the total time playing video games doubled in the U.S. adult population. Furthermore, this data is likely to vastly underreport actual game usage: it excludes children 12 and younger, and it most likely also misses social and mobile players who don't think of themselves as gamers (but nonetheless play games). Actually, Facebook reports that players of its site's games spend an average of $50 a year to play them. A Today's Gamer Survey from 2010 found that $25.3 billion was spent on game play the previous year, a number that is clearly on the rise.

Simultaneously, leisure time has been on the decline, and so has consumption of traditional media. These trends strongly suggest that games have been cannibalizing other forms of entertainment. If you project these consumption trends forward by 15 to 20 years, it becomes clear that games will soon dominate other forms of entertainment. Unsurprisingly, this dovetails with the rise in economic influence of game-crazed millennials whose worldview will radically reshape every aspect of work, commerce, civic life, and recreation as we know it.

So it seems that the deck is stacked irretrievably against business as usual. Classic models of engagement will no longer scale in a world dominated by extreme multitasking and increasing numbers of gamelike distractions. In this new environment, humans will come to expect heightened rewards, stimulation, and feedback. What's exciting today is likely to seem pallid tomorrow, and it will happen before we can even imagine what the future of excitement holds.

How can we possibly reconcile this immense challenge with employee and customer engagement strategies?

Finding the answer requires an acceptance of three deeply interrelated and meaningful truths:

1. The world will not return to the calm, focused ways of the past. Employee and customer multitasking is here to stay.

2. Engagement is the most valuable resource your employees and customers have to give. Your success or failure will be based on how much of it you get.

3. The best way to beat the competition is to make your employee and customer experience as fun and engaging as possible.

In essence, the solution lies in fighting fire with fire. As the world becomes more gamified—through demographic and cultural trends—your organization must do the same. The deeper this understanding penetrates your strategy, the more successful you will be in capturing engagement.

Without engagement, the war is lost before the battles for talent or market share are even fought.

Gamification presents the best tools humanity has ever invented to create and sustain engagement in people. And the world's best organizations—including Nike, SAP, Pearson, Salesforce, Cisco, United Airlines, Microsoft, Target, Spotify, Siemens, GE, IBM, McDonald's, and hundreds more—are increasingly using these techniques to challenge competitors, reimagine their strategies, deliver unprecedented loyalty, and recruit, retain, and drive exceptional achievers and innovators.

If you—like Teddy Roosevelt—view games and play as superfluous to business, it's time to set aside your fears. If you have already seen how gaming is changing the landscape of business, it's time to start applying what you know to improve facets of your company. Now, you must rethink your organization's strategy from the top down and from the bottom up. As you'll see in this book, there are practical ways to use these approaches that work in almost any setting. And while our examples, language, and design patterns are very new, gamification has been going on for hundreds, if not thousands, of years. It's a proven approach using breakthroughs in technology and design to vastly improve the world as we know it—and deliver the organizational success you desire.

Welcome to the Revolution. It will be gamified.

GAMIFY YOUR READ

Throughout the book you will see boxes like this one featuring this symbol:

It signals that a challenge awaits you—if you choose to take it. However, if you don't feel like playing or just don't care to play, your reading (and hopefully enjoyment) of this *will not suffer*. Simply ignore the boxes and game indicators, and keep on reading.

For those of you who like the idea of adding an additional element of excitement to your read, we salute you.

It is our hope that these opportunities will help to illustrate some of the mechanics leveraged by gamification, as well as motivate engaged reading, create happy readers, and also prove that with the right amount of creativity, *anything can be gamified*.

Good luck, and if you are ready to read: On your marks, get set—Go!

PART I

GAMIFICATION AS
WINNING STRATEGY

1

THE REVOLUTION WILL BE GAMIFIED

★

Napoléon's Winning Game

When Napoléon invaded Egypt after the French Revolution, one in seven sailors could expect to develop—and eventually die from—scurvy. This deadly form of malnutrition had been the scourge of travelers for thousands of years, and despite Napoléon's successes, his military was still vulnerable to it. At-sea rations for the men tended toward the filling rather than the nutrient rich, and they were composed mostly of salted meats and weevil-ridden flour. For land-based troops, the problem was no less severe. War operations had the daunting task of securing rations for soldiers in enemy territory. This often meant paying colossal sums for food to opportunistic merchants and using other tactics necessary to secure supply lines.

What Napoléon needed was a way to keep food fresh and nutritious, but also transportable. France was a major agricultural power, after all, and along with its annexed territories, it could readily produce the entire nutritional needs of the country's far-flung armies. So if the country's farmers could produce the food

GAMIFY YOUR READ

Chapterwide Scavenger Hunt

"Collect" the following items as you read through the chapter. Then "bring" them to *The Gamification Revolution* app at http://gamrev.com and join the conversation! You may also verify your answers by visiting the answer key at the back of the book.

➤ Find the name of the man whose idea won Napoléon's Food Preservation Prize.

➤ Find one thing devotees of the McDonald's *Monopoly* game claim they do to win.

➤ Find and name everyone's biggest competitor according to this chapter.

➤ Find the percentage of people, in light of a 2009 study, who play computer and/or video games on a regular basis.

➤ Who is the "average gamer," according to this chapter?

➤ A Common Sense Media (CSM) study showed that 23 percent of what age group uses more than one technology medium at a time?

➤ In order to bring progression to mastery into your organization in a meaningful way, what should you design first?

➤ Name one meaningful game mechanic mentioned in this chapter.

consumed by French soldiers, Napoléon's power and reach would grow exponentially.

Emperor Bonaparte could have simply asked his fellow countrymen to hand over *their ideas* for the good of the military. After all, "love of country" has been a motivational mainstay during times of war throughout history and across borders. However, the number and quality of good ideas may have been limited if motivated by patriotism alone. Similarly, Napoléon might have conducted a headhunt, seeking out qualified candidates to employ in his food preservation project. But doing so would certainly have cost time and money—both of which were precious during wartime.

So Napoléon did something revolutionary: he proposed a game.

In 1795 he offered 12,000 francs to the invention that could solve the food preservation problem, thereby launching a *grand challenge* that enthralled the middle class and scientific elite of France. Just over a decade later, a 61-year-old Parisian confectioner, Nicolas Appert, stepped forward with the solution that won the prize. His relatively simple approach involved heating food within an airtight container. Appert's discovery, largely similar to the basic canning process still in use today, made it possible to preserve fresh fruits, meats, and vegetables, which changed the lives of soldiers, sailors, and ultimately, all of humanity.

Whether or not Appert or someone else would have developed the technique on his own in spite of the game, we'll never know. However, the Food Preservation Prize was a rousing success for Napoléon, although it came too late to save his armies from defeat a few years later. In the 200 years since, the rest of us have gained immeasurably from the breakthrough with profound improvements in our nutritional health, thanks to the accessibility of safe food. (Appert himself lived into his nineties.) But beyond the crowning of a winner, the real success of grand challenge designs lies in their process and ancillary benefits:

➤ *Discovery.* Grand challenges solicit results from unexpected corners, including nonscientists and nonacademics, which raises the odds of obtaining truly novel approaches.

➤ *Optionality.* A grand challenge delivers dozens of solutions at no incremental cost. By comparison, structured research typically requires funding for each possible solution path.

➤ *Cost arbitrage.* Because the winners also usually receive major status and attention for having achieved public success, we don't need to pay them as much as we would under other circumstances.

Napoléon's grand challenge is an example of *gamification*: the use of game thinking and game mechanics to engage people and solve problems—though it obviously predates the word by over a century. It also happened to be the perfect gamified design to solve the kind of problem the emperor had identified. Napoléon was far from the first person (or last) to design a grand challenge. Dozens of major advances have been generated in a similar fashion, including: determining longitude (1714), making the first flight across the Atlantic (1927), and launching the first privately manned spaceflight (2004)—just to name a few. And while the use of competition to drive extraordinary achievement is commonplace, it is not as easy as it seems, nor is it appropriate for every situation.

There are six core types of gamified approaches to driving engagement and problem solving. They can be used individually or together, and they can be applied to either of the two main stakeholder groups in an organization: customers or employees. The six approaches are listed in the following table.

If you are near a soccer or football field, those kids running by are engaged in a *rapid feedback game.* Your kids or grandkids are probably utilizing *simulation-discovery games* in their classroom at school. You are very likely engaging in some kind of *status marathon* when you go on social networking websites, waiting for "likes," "comments," and new contacts. In fact, status marathons are often central to such "gamified" systems as career tracks (from raises to promotions), religions (with titles indicating levels of importance like a "priest" or a "deacon" in Catholicism), and politics (rising through the ranks from city council to president). Meanwhile, frequent-flier members are regularly engaged in a *commercial/negotiation system* when they try to earn virtual currency in the form of "miles." And people everywhere—from business

Game Type	Description
Grand challenges	These are highly publicized competitions usually awarding cash prizes, and they are designed to solve a specific problem of a complex or indeterminate nature.
Rapid feedback systems	These are gamified systems whereby feedback—such as scoring—shapes behavior in real time.
Simulation-discovery	Principally designed for educational purposes, these games allow for the exploration of new ideas, models, and/or scenarios.
Status marathons	These long-arc systems use status ladders and rewards. Most customer loyalty programs strive to embody this approach.
Commercial/negotiation	These rely heavily on a virtual or real-world economy including markets and auctions. *Monopoly* is a great example of this modality.
Expressive	These games are designed to facilitate creativity, individuality, and emotional satisfaction in users.

managers to school administrators to organizations that host question-and-answer websites on the Internet—are looking for ways to engage others in some kind of *expressive game*.

As you can see, these gamification patterns are all around us, and many have been for centuries. They are not new concepts. However, we have developed new frameworks, technologies, and design patterns to make them scalable and truly effective. While each one of these approaches is powerful, the key to successfully driving engagement is knowing when—and how—to deploy the right one. Fundamentally, it's all about matching the solution to the audience.

Growing Your Audience

Growing an audience is what McDonald's had in mind when in 1987 it launched its now famous *Monopoly* game. During the once-a-year promotional period, the company offers customers ordering specific

What Is Engagement?

Engagement can mean many things to many people, but the following indicators can create meaning around engagement in quantifiable terms:

Recency. How long ago did the users last visit?
Frequency. How often do they visit in a period of time?
Duration. When do they come, and how long do they stay?
Virality. How many people do they refer?
Ratings. When asked directly, how do they rate their experience?
Knowledge. If quizzed, how much do they know about the correlating product or brand?

The importance of these metrics varies depending on your users and market focus. For example, virality might be relatively unimportant for an internal enterprise resource planning (ERP) system, but it could be very important for a consumer-facing customer acquisition campaign. Regardless of which numbers signal success for your business, it's critical that you understand your baseline and objectives before executing any gamified programs. Your likelihood of success increases proportionately with shared agreement on the key metrics—what those metrics are, how they are collected, and what they mean to the organization.

menu items game pieces mirroring those found in the Parker Brothers' board game of the same name. When it comes to the value meals, the larger the size ordered, the more chances to win.

The game is the company's largest promotional project each year, and indeed it is the largest promotion in the fast-food and quick-serve restaurant industry as a whole. People who play the game claim they enjoy not just the immediate chance to win menu items with every purchase but also the long-term strategizing necessitated by a game that encourages players to collect whole sets, or "monopolies." This harder-to-accomplish goal awards big-ticket prizes like vacations and cars, as well as a million-dollar grand prize.

Devotees of the game claim to travel not just within their own cities and states to various McDonald's restaurants but also to McDonald's restaurants far away in the hopes of finding winning game pieces. Furthermore, some consumers admit that they are more likely to visit McDonald's more often, as well as increase the size of their orders, so that they can amass a greater number of game pieces. These same players admit that they will do so even if they are not hungry for the additional food they order. In other words, they will spend money to buy food they intend to throw away for the sake of the game. Countless articles describe strategies for winning, and they make suggestions for where to find the pieces you most want. Since 2003 the play has gone online, making the game's engagement factor even stickier. In a 2008 interview with *Promo Magazine*, Chris Hess, VP of the Marketing Store (the ad agency responsible for the game), said, "We've found that when people play the online *Monopoly* game, there's a level of consumer engagement that keeps them coming back."

The *Monopoly* game—one of the most successful and longest-running gamified projects in the customer-facing world—is a good example of a gamified system leading to an impressive level of customer engagement. It targets a desire to explore (finding the next game piece), and it helps to create value and profit from a virtual currency (trading and even buying missing properties, while technically against the rules, is not uncommon). *Monopoly* at McDonald's has driven marginal customers to its stores, and it has raised incremental spending among the restaurant's loyalists. According to the company, the game itself was responsible for a 5.5 percent same-store revenue lift in a single month in the fourth quarter of 2011. This equates to approximately $350 million in incremental revenue over the 60 days of the promotion.

From a game.

Monopoly: Not Just Any Game

Originally conceived in 1903 as an anticapitalist teaching tool, *Monopoly* went through dozens of iterations before landing in its current form as one of the most popular games in history. Although the game creators' initial strident message is mostly buried in the version you know today, the design reason behind the object of the game—that one person wins absolutely while everyone else goes bankrupt—should now make more sense.

But this ubiquitous board game, translated into dozens of languages and being the source of so many screaming matches, is also a powerful force in teaching. Tim Vandenberg, a nationally ranked competitive *Monopoly* player, uses it to drive extraordinary math results from elementary school students at his troubled school in California's Inland Empire. To find out how he has produced top-scoring math students, watch his video on the companion app to *The Gamification Revolution* at http://gamrev.com. While you are there, you can also explore related media; access Twitter and web links; unlock exclusive content; interact with your peers, colleagues, and friends; and make notes for yourself.

From Napoléon's nineteenth-century Food Preservation Prize to McDonald's twenty-first-century *Monopoly* game, some of the best solutions have been gamified. These two examples, and the dozens that follow in subsequent chapters, herald *The Gamification Revolution*, where the power of games is being harnessed to build the enterprises of the future. By looking at case studies from leading organizations, businesses, and governments with games already in play and those on the horizon, we will explore all the ways games can better strengthen everything about your business from reinventing your strategic process to raising employee engagement, innovation, and wellness while driving customer loyalty and community.

If You Can't Beat 'Em, Learn What Works and Use It

When Premal Shah, CEO of Kiva, a nonprofit that helps facilitate microlending in the developing world, was asked who his biggest competition was, his answer was simple:

Zynga.

Yes, that Zynga. The very same Zynga whose name appears as you are waiting for your *Words With Friends* app to open on your iPad. The very same company that's behind the social and casual games that reinvented the genre on social networks and mobile devices. So, you might wonder, is Kiva on the verge of launching the next great social networking–based lending game? Is it in the throes of developing some kind of investment-based soccer league? Because, if not, what does an international microlender have to fear from the social games developer Zynga?

A lot, as Shah understands, because not only is Zynga Kiva's biggest competitor, it is everyone's.

And the biggest competitor isn't just Zynga, PopCap, Gameloft, QQ, or any of the other dozen high-flying social game superstars, but rather games as a whole. People are playing in epidemic numbers—from the casual games they use to unwind between meetings (such as *Tetris* or the previously mentioned *Words With Friends*) to the *massively multiplayer online games*, also called MMOGs, they play at night in lieu of sleeping (such as the community-based *World of Warcraft*) to the console games they play to the detriment of their social lives (such as the violent but popular *Call of Duty*). And while those players might be thinking about accruing points, winning prizes, or advancing on a leaderboard, they are *not* thinking about your brand or product.

What's more, mobile games, especially social and casual games (like *Angry Birds, Cut the Rope,* and *Tiny Wings*), are rapidly taking over where console and MMOGs once were king. A recent study from MocoSpace found that while 80 percent of social gamers play while commuting or waiting to begin appointments, a whopping 96 percent admit that they are playing these games at home, from their couch, bed, or front porch. In 2009, the research firm TNS Global reported that over 60 percent of the population in the western world—including the United States—played computer and/or video games on a regular basis. These hundreds of millions of players—and their numbers are growing all the time—are changing the way we think about the games and the gamers, and they are demanding a more gamelike experience from the rest of their world.

No matter what you think of games, and regardless of the prognosis for specific game developers like Zynga, their core achievement is undeniable: they have driven an extraordinary amount of engagement, clearly to the detriment of all other activities. And this trend is accelerating.

Your Customer Is Changing

In 2012 cable provider Optimum (the New York division of Cable-Vision) aired a television commercial that featured three generations of a family using Optimum services to stay in touch. The college-age son lamented being beaten by his grandmother while playing a word game with her. His mother, meanwhile, let out an exasperated laugh as she talked about how she had been trying to get her mother online for years and that it wasn't until the senior citizen took up online gaming that any headway could be made. Finally, the feisty old matriarch revealed that it wasn't until the games came along that the experience of learning how to use the Internet held any appeal for her.

While grandmothers might not be the number one gaming demographic just yet, their numbers are steadily on the rise. Casual game leader PopCap commissioned a study in late 2010, and the study revealed something that many women could have told you: the average gamer is no longer a 13- to 34-year-old male. She is a 43-year-old woman. And things are no different in the rapidly growing mobile channel. Flurry, the mobile analytics firm, found that women are 53 percent more likely to be playing games than men—up to three times per day on average.

The spread of games to a wider population than ever before is an even bigger story—the long-term demographic shift is in fact propelling us toward an ever more gamelike future. In fact, as more women and seniors take up gaming, so do those demographics you most expect to play games. Teens, it turns out, are not only playing games, they are *living* them. And it is this fundamental shift in their behavior that has them leading the trend toward gamification—and making its arrival an inevitability.

How to Land a Plane Without Experience

Walk down any street and you'll pass dozens of kids like Remy, a 12-year-old of average height, looks, and demeanor. There's not much to distinguish him from any other tween you'll notice in your neighborhood. You might even call him unremarkable—that is, until he lands a commercial airliner with virtually no instruction or training.

Filmed for the TV series *The Aviators*, Remy was brought in off the street to a professional flight simulator facility. With minimal instruction, he was asked to bring a Boeing 737 down for a simulated landing at the Los Angeles airport (LAX) using visual flight conditions without the assistance of an autopilot—a task that only pilots with thousands of hours of literal experience get to do in the real world. Within minutes, and without any training, Remy safely brought the aircraft to a halt on the apron at one of the world's busiest airports.

For those of us who fly regularly, this is an astounding story. How can a child with no experience do something that adult professionals with extensive experience find so challenging? Can flying a plane really be that easy or intuitive, or is there something else going on? The answer comes from the owner of the simulator facility in an aside to the producers: "They [tweens] pick up on this quite quickly... because they have their computer and video game experiences, so this becomes like second nature to them."

Today's kids are being raised on games, a reality that is profoundly changing both their brains and our world. From before some can talk, they are learning how to interact with technology, in many cases through games. This long-simmering trend has picked up steam since the advent of iOS devices like iPads and other mobile technologies. Common Sense Media (CSM) research has shown that a staggering 70 percent of parents allow their toddlers and young kids to use them. Further, CSM research has also shown that as of 2010, 38 percent of all kids under the age of eight have used a smartphone or tablet, including 10 percent of children under the age of one. Whether or not you agree with the choices of their parents, there is no choice other than to face facts: these are how the employees and consumers of tomorrow are being raised. There's no better time than now to get into the game.

Much of the momentum is being fueled by the powerful bond between young kids and games, which was well established even before Apple launched its first iPhone in 2007. But as a result of these games and the mobile technologies that have allowed them to become ubiquitous, today's kids are smarter, better coordinated, and better able to multitask than ever before. The same CSM study showed that 23 percent of five- to eight-year-olds use more than one technology medium at a time—suggesting that by the time this generation comes of age, they will need more stimulation and excitement than any other generation in history. This need—and their evolving brains—will change our world, whether we're ready for it or not.

Somewhere near the top of those changes will be a move toward products that provide today's kids—tomorrow's adults—with deeper and more meaningful interactions. They will seek these interactions through entertainment and engagement, with games and game mechanics becoming the expectation rather than an exception woven through most facets of their lives. It will be up to each of us to provide them with it, or you can be certain that they will find it somewhere else. And with kids as intuitively smart as Remy, you certainly won't be able to hold them back for long.

Cutting Through the Noise

The landscape of customer interactions increasingly resembles some of the world's most distracting places. The flashing lights, blaring sounds, and enticing advertisements of Times Square, Shibuya, and Picadilly Circus are no longer unusual or confined to large public intersections. They are everywhere—in your pocket, on your monitor, in your ear. And don't forget daily distractions coming from work or school and family! As the noise increases, your strategic challenge won't be to grow louder than the competition. It will be to cut through the noise. You will be summoned to create a bubble of silence, a way to focus your employees and customers that enables them to hear what you have to say, what you need them to do, and what will be best for you and what will be best for them. As it turns out, nothing does this better than gamification.

The best strategy isn't to beat game companies on a level playing field. You will never be as good as a Zynga, Rovio, PopCap, or Blizzard at making games. The best way to win in this challenge is to take the best elements of games, loyalty programs, and behavioral economics and weave them together with the most powerful elements of your brand.

You aren't going to make games. You're going to make games work for you.

Driving Performance with Mastery

Great gamified experiences, like great games, invest heavily in cultivating a sense of mastery—and progression toward it at all times. Systems like Weight Watchers or Alcoholics Anonymous use this concept well by offering points for food in the case of the former and badges and levels in the case of the latter. Most of the games you've played, whether you've noticed or not, make mastery central to their value proposition.

Mastery is different from winning—although it's easy to confuse the two. Winning is really about achieving a goal, while mastery is about acquiring knowledge and demonstrating control and doing so in a steady and consistent progression. Put another way, mastery is a continuous improvement process, whereas winning is a destination. Because few people can win but an unlimited number of people can achieve mastery, a focus on the latter gives us the potential to make more of our employees and customers happy—and they are happier longer.

In order to bring *progression to mastery* into your organization in a meaningful way, you need to design the key mechanics:

- ➤ A goal
- ➤ Markers toward the goal (for example, levels)
- ➤ Constant reinforcement of progress (points, typically)
- ➤ Social reinforcement
- ➤ Logical progression of difficulty
- ➤ Side challenges and different experiences to hold interest

These mechanics are elemental to most great game and gamification designs (see also Figure 1.1). Now consider how well your overall organizational structure hews to these principles. Can new employees see a clear goal for their own development despite knowing that they may not ultimately be the CEO? Is there a logical progression of difficulty? Do you do a good job of marking progress?

Most organizations haven't brought this level of game thinking or design discipline to their overall environment. But some have combined the power of mastery with other gamification approaches to radically reimagine their workplaces and drive unprecedented performance.

In his seminal book *A Theory of Fun,* entrepreneur and game designer Raph Koster posits that mastery is the main thing that

FIGURE 1.1 To move users from a progression to mastery, you need to construct a gamified system that moves them through these six steps.

makes games fun in the first place. Nicole Lazzaro, expert game designer, expands on this theory with her "4 Keys 2 Fun." In her groundbreaking research, Lazzaro shows that mastery (or "hard fun" in her parlance) is one of the most important parts of good design. It is this belief in the reward of mastery for the sake of mastery that makes it such a powerful driver.

Progressing to mastery can be seen in slow-learning-curve games—for example, *Bejeweled* or *Angry Birds*—where fun yet simple behaviors are repeated until players increase in skill level (see Figure 1.2). In other words, the games are designed to carefully move users up to expertise through a series of levels of increasing difficulty that train and entertain. As players progress through the levels and begin to accomplish things in the game, the experience (and their investment in it) becomes more fun and more important.

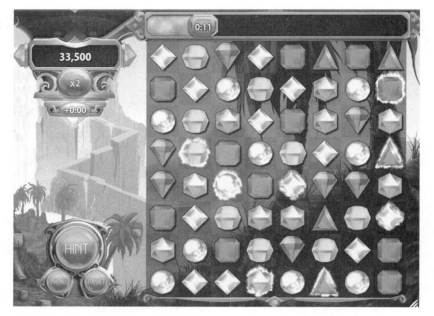

FIGURE 1.2 In the *Bejeweled Blitz* game, players have to match multiple gems to receive the highest score. The game may seem simple, but mechanics like mastery, challenge, points, and levels are finely tuned to maximize engagement.

What Gamification Is

When governments, businesses, and organizations of all sizes and types embrace game thinking and mechanics, they are better able to engage their audiences, cut through the noise, drive innovation, and ultimately increase their revenue.

The process of implementing these games and strategies into business is called *gamification*, and with it you can build experiences that will provide built-in meaning and trigger the motivation of employees and customers. *Gamified design* leverages the best of game design, loyalty program design, and behavioral economics to solve critical problems and drive engagement.

Game mechanics are the basic elements that make up games, and they include *points, badges (achievements), levels, leaderboards,* and *rewards.* Together, these elements are combined to deliver a *system of mastery* to end users—in other words, they serve as guide posts toward "winning." Using concepts that are *intrinsically* and *extrinsically motivating*, gamification is about finding—and delivering—fun and enjoyment in a wide range of contexts. A basic description of the key mechanics follows.

Points

Points are systems used to track behavior, keep score, and provide feedback. There are multiple kinds of point systems, from very broadly adopted (and well-understood) checking account balance systems to much less common systems like school district technology preparedness systems. (Later in the book we outline the Department of Education's successful *Reach to the Top* game.) Point systems can serve a wide range of functions, and they are typically divided into five different kinds:

> - *XP.* Experience points track your experience over time.
> - *Redeemable.* These are currency points that you can earn and redeem.
> - *Reputation.* Just like transactions that count toward your credit score, these points contribute to establishing your reputation.
> - *Skill.* These points denote your ability in a specific area.
> - *Karma.* These points that you earn for helping others are nonredeemable.

Using the right point architecture for the right function can be challenging, but fundamentally all gamified systems begin with an XP point system. Even if you don't have a virtual currency, XP helps you track—and provide feedback on—user behavior over time. This and other essential functions of point systems are products of our intrinsic desire to keep score (and share feedback), and they are critical gamification tools in shaping behavior.

Badges (Achievements)

Badges are tokens that represent the achievement of a particular goal. Within game design, they are part of the generic category "achievements," along with trophies and other symbols of accomplishment. Badges have always been a popular part of gamification—even before modern technology—with the military, the Girl Scouts, and other organizations making heavy use of the concept. What makes all kinds of achievements compelling is that earning them gives the user an opportunity to feel successful and accomplished, which generates a touch point for the gamified system to communicate with the users, bringing them back into the experience.

Moreover, badges allow users to show off their accomplishments to others and to keep track of what they've done. Some users may also exhibit a strong desire to collect, and badges allow them to create and complete sets and/or collections.

No matter which badging model you choose, the badges should be well designed and authentic to maximize user adoption and interest.

Levels

Levels are structured hierarchies of progress, usually represented by ascending numbers or values (for example, bronze, silver, and gold). Levels exist to provide users with a sense of progress and accomplishment, acting as a shorthand for the points achieved in a given system (for example, bachelor's, master's, and doctorate degrees). When paired with a "map of the world" to indicate the meaning behind the level—where the level exists on the spectrum and how to go higher or fall lower, respectively—levels can be useful for roughly explaining how the system of progress works and what users can expect to achieve if they continue within it.

Clearly, levels and badges have a great deal of overlap, and many systems that leverage badges don't necessarily incorporate levels, and vice versa. However, they are powerful tools that are especially useful when designing a system with a great deal of intrinsic structure, like workplace hierarchies.

Leaderboards

Also known as *scoreboards, leaderboards* are designed to show a ranked list of users in descending order from highest scoring to lowest scoring. Because they are so ingrained in our culture, they provide a clear and instantaneous understanding of rank, which can be a powerful incentive. They can also act as a powerful disincentive, particularly if they show only the top 10 or 20 players at a time. Those at the lower rungs or those just entering the game might find themselves less motivated by an apparent lack of mobility in the system.

As gamified systems generally reveal their complexity in measured ways, this issue is amplified because users don't know how long or hard they will have to engage before reaching the top. Ergo, today's top leaderboards have become social and relative, usually placing the player in the middle of the rankings (instead of at their absolute rank) and more regularly amid their friends and contacts. Because players feel like there is potential for mobility, this design offers a better incentive for them to reengage. On the other hand, supercompetitive players, as well as team-based environments, tend to be more amenable to straightforward leaderboards, benefiting from the competitive spirit they provoke.

Rewards

One of the most important elements of a gamified system—and certainly the one that gets a lot of attention—is *rewards*. Broadly speaking, rewards can be categorized into *intrinsic* versus *extrinsic*—that is, self-generated versus externally delivered. The goal of a good gamified system is to offer a set of rewards that activates the users' intrinsic desires, while leveraging external incentives and pressure where appropriate. The clearest model for understanding these elements of reward programs is described in the acronym SAPS:

Status. Utilizing such tools as titles and color-coded levels

Access. Providing exclusive opportunities to engage, like lunch with the CEO or celebrity autographs

Power. Exercising control over others in the real or virtual world—a team leader, for example

Stuff. Offering free things including giveaways, cash, or gift cards

This list of potential rewards to users is in order of most meaningful to least meaningful, stickiest to least sticky, and cheapest to most expensive. One of the benefits of hewing to this approach in gamification is a substantial reduction in hard costs from incentive programs. Gamified systems lean heavily on psychological and virtual rewards for driving meaningful behavior, while standard incentive systems like to offer cash and prizes (stuff). As you'll see in many of the examples profiled in this book, a large number of gamified systems have achieved incredible results with minimal or no cash incentives. The key is to build alignment between the players, the company, and the system.

What Gamification Isn't

Gamification, as we'll see, is about much more than just game mechanics like points and badges. It's equally important, however, to define what gamification is *not*. First and foremost, gamification is *not* about just throwing game mechanics at a problem in the hope that engagement will improve as a result; instead, you must design a thoughtful and meaningful experience. Second, gamification is *not* solely about coming up with cool, innovative, and virtual rewards; rather, incentives are important, but they are not the whole picture. Last, gamification is *not* about making everything into a game. As this book will amply illustrate, we need to use only the best ideas and mechanics from games—not the gamey-ness itself—to have the desired effect. So rest assured, you don't need to build a laser tag room off of your cafeteria. There are other ways to build fun and engagement without taking things to an extreme. (Not that we're discouraging laser tag rooms...)

Think about gamifying your company, system, or process like icing on a cake. If the underlying cake is tasteless and/or poorly executed, no amount of frosting will fix the problem. Gamification and the entire engagement layer are essential elements of the whole, and as the top layer, they serve as an invitation to eat the cake. But remember, people will not take a second bite if the cake is bad, nor will they be excited to keep eating if the icing doesn't do its job to complement the cake. The key is to make it all work together—one delicious cake made complete by a layer of inviting frosting on top.

Critically, games are not synonymous with winning—and arriving at a "winner" is seldom the goal of gamification. Consider some of the most enduring and popular MMOGs of all time, such as *World of Warcraft*, *Final Fantasy XI*, or *Happy Farm* (with over 23 million players in 2011, *Happy Farm* is the world's most popular MMOG). The average MMOG player dedicates 21 hours a week to his or her game. While there are goals within the game, winning—in the classic "beat the boss level" sense—is not the objective. In fact, in some ways, winning can even spoil the fun—especially if socializing with your group is the main source of enjoyment in the game. To that end, gamification ideally seeks to develop steady game play over long periods of time, drawing players back in to play time and time again for enjoyable and engaging experiences.

Committing to Gamification

By implementing one or more of the gamified strategies found in this book, you can grow the value of your company exponentially among your consumers and your employees. By doing so, you can vault your organization into the elite tier of best-in-class companies that are transforming the world. You will position yourself to dominate the battle for talent, customers, and engagement in the attention-starved culture. In the coming chapters, we'll illustrate

how winners win with gamification and how they overcame challenges to create world-class organizations and relationships.

Begin by creating opportunities for your organization to thrive
in this new environment. The following list of basic agreements
will help facilitate the shift:

1. A commitment to fostering engagement as the key to success
2. A belief that *lasting* engagement takes both time and effort to
   maintain
3. An understanding that engagement precedes—not follows—
   customer revenue
4. The view that your employees are also customers of your
   company (its brand, demands, and so on)

Beginning with these basics, the lessons of *The Gamification
Revolution* can help you create, sustain, and grow your competitive
advantage with both employees and customers. While most examples of transformative gamification have begun with very modest
program objectives, increasingly a strategic view of gamification is
emerging. To prepare your organization for the coming changes in
the market, and also to more fully leverage the benefits of gamification tactically, developing a workable strategy is critical.

GAMIFICATION AS WINNING CORPORATE STRATEGY

★

How Social Networking Is Killing the Car

In the past, when most people turned 16, they couldn't wait to drive. That little piece of paper signaling the legal right to do so served as a sign of freedom from parents, freedom to travel, and

GAMIFY YOUR READ

Question and Answer

Collect the one-word answers to the questions sprinkled throughout the chapter in Gamify Your Read. Plug all of the words into *The Gamification Revolution* app, which can be accessed at http://gamrev.com to unlock your achievement and access supplemental materials. You may also verify your answers by visiting the answer key at the back of the book.

freedom to play music loudly. But recently, research from major automakers has uncovered a shocking revelation: today's kids don't really care about driving. According to Frontier Group and U.S. PIRG, the number of miles driven by teens fell more than 23 percent from 2001 to 2010, while the number of young adults without a driver's license increased by 20 percent to include over a quarter of the eligible population.

Of course, the freedom and control of the driving experience have remained intact. However, if given the choice, kids don't want to be the one behind the wheel. Reasons for this shift are many including an increased environmental and urban consciousness and/or better public transit systems. But within the data lies a clue to the big motivator, amplified by private auto industry research: the real problem is that driving isn't *fun enough* anymore.

Until recently, the purpose of a vehicle to most young people has been to create connections within their social sphere. Today, by using social media, multiplayer games, and e-commerce, many of these interactions can be conducted digitally instead of in person, eliminating long drives around town. The digital approach is not only greener and cheaper but it is also more immediately positively reinforced (consider how many texts or likes you can receive during a 10-minute ride). Meanwhile, through peer, parental, and punitive pressure, today's drivers are discouraged from multitasking while driving, which means no texting, no social networking, no flirting, and certainly no game playing. While their smartphones buzz incessantly in their laps, with notifications, pokes, music, and game moves waiting for responses, they are expected to keep their eyes on the road ahead. So, as it turns out, not only is driving itself less intrinsically rewarding than social media or games, but it's actually in conflict with them.

When it comes to public safety, the prohibition on multitasking is an important one. According to research from the U.S. Department of Transportation, texting while driving increases the risk of an accident by a factor of 23, with younger drivers posing an elevated risk due to both inexperience as well as even more opportunities for distraction while behind the wheel as compared to the rest of the population. And the probability is that driving will continue to become *less cool* over time, with more and more kids calling out "shotgun" and leaving the driving to someone else—as long as there is a qualified *someone else.*

Perhaps in the process of making driving safer by eliminating multitasking from the equation, society might end up making the automobile less attractive as a means of transportation. What if, at the same time, the opportunities for multitasking—like social and gamified alternatives—continue to increase in quality, reach, and meaningfulness? What effect will this shift have on the auto industry in the long term?

While automakers have had to contend with many challenges over the last 50 years—including an increased emphasis on safety and the environment, elevated manufacturing costs, and foreign competition—one thing they could always count on was the steady public *desire* for cars. Perhaps in the future, thanks to gamified changes in the interactive landscape, people will choose Facebook and *Farmville* over the family Ford. How will our lives, cities, and society change? More urgently, what will the auto industry do about it?

This strategic shift in human behavior and the competitive response to it—if driven by games and gamification—will require a new organization of thought processes. It will not be enough to respond to the threat and opportunity of a distracted population by offering one-time-winner sweepstakes or employee-of-the-month challenges (though both have their place). To compete successfully and to position your organization to win in this new landscape, gamification must permeate your whole company from top to bottom.

In short, you need a strategy.

While the auto industry hasn't solved its yawning motivation gap yet, it is taking concrete steps to address this issue using gamification. Honda, Toyota, Nissan, and Ford have developed *in-dash experiences* that leverage the power of gamification to engage

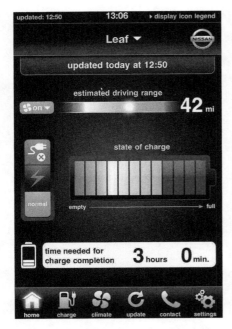

FIGURE 2.1 The Nissan Leaf includes a dashboard interface that allows drivers to compare safe and ecologically sound driving practices to those of other drivers, making the experience a social one.

audiences in a whole new environmentally aware and safety-conscious way. For example, Ford has leveraged the game concept of virtual pets (or *Tamagotchi*) to make driving more fun. In their Focus/Fusion hybrid, a virtual plant grows green and lush as drivers make ecologically sound choices such as driving more slowly to conserve gas. The plant offers feedback and positive reinforcement for every single mile driven. The *Nissan Leaf* takes the concept one step further, making use of Facebook to allow drivers to compete against each other to become the best, safest, and greenest (Figure 2.1).

The company offers challenges and feedback to create not only better drivers but also proud and engaged drivers of the *Nissan Leaf*. This kind of innovative design is the right first step for Detroit. With further investment, there's no telling how automakers could reimagine the driving experience.

Strategic Approaches to Gamification

From innovative product concepts like in-dash games to entirely game-based projects and businesses, smart companies in the automotive industry and beyond are developing overarching gamification strategies to help them adapt and thrive in this changing environment. Some have leveraged it on the ground floor, while others have used it to re-energize or turn around a business going sideways. In every case, the strategic value of gamification highlights some of the ways that it is so powerful. Some of the more inspirational examples are driving some strategic visions forward with a velocity never before seen.

As always, there are some recurring patterns within those examples of companies that have succeeded with a gamification strategy. These patterns include the following:

- Orienting around the user
- Hiring a chief engagement officer
- Giving users what they want
- Making engagement the number one job
- Knowing when the game is the thing
- Creating a center of excellence and innovation

Let's examine these concepts in greater depth.

Orienting Around the User

In 2004, eBay was one of the giants of the Internet—riding high on the strength of its dominance in e-commerce as well as its charismatic CEO, Meg Whitman. But by 2008, the company had fallen on hard times, its stock trading nearly 80 percent off its peak. Many analysts questioned whether it could survive poor decisions like its $2.5 billion Skype acquisition and the constant drubbing by merchants who were annoyed at Whitman's drive to increase fees and squeeze their margins.

But by 2012, the company had engineered what most on Wall Street thought was impossible—the turnaround of an Internet giant. In the second quarter of that year, the company posted record earnings fueled by mobile successes and a new checkout design. Even the "irreparable" auctions and commerce business had had its best quarter since 2006, posting $6.3 billion in sales volume.

While some credit has to go to the company's PayPal and mobile divisions, which were stellar performers in the early years of the millennium, another, less public hero also helped to catalyze this extraordinary achievement: eBay's reorientation around user-centric design.

To hear Matt Maclaurin, leader of eBay's EPIC design lab, tell it, the most important thing the company has done is to prioritize user needs over corporate objectives. This means borrowing heavily from game companies like Rockstar (makers of the popular *Grand Theft Auto* series). One concept that has made the leap from the world of entertainment to the world of commerce is the notion of building teams to design, engineer, and execute user-focused projects at scale, quickly and with highly flexible tools.

For example, in a games company, teams are often formed to tackle a specific design challenge. The teams bring together designers, engineers, project managers, and businesspeople to solve problems quickly. The temporary nature of the group allows for creative and flexible problem solving. The teams are then mixed into other teams working on alternate project elements. They are typically given powerful design tools and an infrastructure that allows them to scale their efforts to the needs of the business.

For eBay, implementing this structural and design shift was made possible because as an organization, it has gaming deeply embedded in its DNA—after all, the gamified experience of an auction is at the heart of the eBay shopping experience. The development of a *feedback score* used to indicate the trustworthiness of vendors based on the behaviors of their customers (repeat business, increased business, and so on) has been a stalwart example of gamification. It was developed explicitly using game designers to make the marketplace more trustworthy and self-policing—in

GAMIFY YOUR READ

Answer in one word: What does eBay's feedback score indicate about a seller?

order to solve the problem of dishonest buyers and sellers who had stunted the company's growth in the early, free-for-all days of the Internet.

To create trust between buyers and sellers, eBay built a reputation system at a scale that hasn't been replicated to this day. By allowing customers to offer feedback on merchant behavior, products, and efficiency, and then quantifying that data, the shopping experience from one merchant to the next can be effectively ranked and valued, helping to drive sales and attract business.

As a result, eBay's hiring plan leans heavily on games, and the company actively recruits from games and gamification fields for a wide range of roles within the organization. This gives eBay a particular advantage in the quest for gamified engagement, and that has not gone unnoticed by other companies.

Hiring a Chief Engagement Officer

Smart organizations like eBay understand that gamification need no longer be relegated to the games industry. As a result, they have started to make it a part of their overall team strategy. Across a wide range of industries—from finance to enterprise software, from porn to packaged goods—companies are not just hiring *from* games. They are hiring *for* gamification. So commonly are games and game systems becoming important parts of corporate culture that a new position has been born: the *chief engagement officer (CNO)*.

Spigit, Cynergy Systems, Nike, and other companies for whom gamification seems to naturally align have hired gamification experts to help craft their product and marketing approaches. More interestingly, companies like Vivid, Yahoo!, SAP, NBC/Universal, and EMC that don't have an obvious link to games have brought games and game designers in house—delegating the design and development functions to an internal champion who looks at gamification as a *key performance indicator* (KPI). In fact, most of the companies profiled in this book have achieved their objectives principally through the drive and motivation of an in-house champion.

Although many of these CNOs (whose titles may differ from company to company) come with game design expertise, this is not a strict requirement. What is consistent about the successful ones is that they are deeply interested in human behavior and, in particular, motivation. Designing to motivate behavior change can be accomplished only with a deep understanding of what motivates human behaviors in the first place. And while from the outside the science might seem solid, it's actually in a great state of flux. New research on behavioral economics, gamification, and loyalty continues to be published monthly, and many of the examples we profile here are so fresh they have yet to be studied in a controlled, academic way.

This means that an organization's success with engagement across all vectors is best informed by an expert who can look closely at the changing data, as well as changing behaviors, for what works and what doesn't. By providing constant insight, drive, and direction, the organization can monitor disparate programs all trying to drive mutually exclusive outcomes. Outsourced vendors and consultants can provide a great deal of the starting energy and technology required to begin progressing down a viable gamified path; however, ultimately enlisting an internal expert will allow all collected knowledge to flourish inside the organization. The drive for engagement—and an understanding of how behavioral design fits that objective—is one of the most critical knowledge resources your organization can nurture and support in the long term.

This chief engagement officer is in a unique role in a company because her focus is to drive engagement—for both (or either) customer-facing and employee-facing elements. The individual must serve as a watchdog for evolving trends and discipline, and she must be able to both directly drive engagement and find the right resources to foster the engagement process. The CNO must be able to build a set of guidelines for the organization to follow in order to remain on message and task from every gamified direction toward which her company turns. This doesn't mean that the CNO is responsible for the day-to-day operations of every gamified app

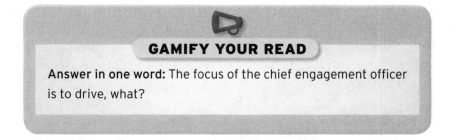

or service. Rather, it means that she is responsible for the creation and ongoing sustenance of engagement strategies throughout the organization.

The role continues to evolve, but no matter how it is structured, one thing of which a strong engagement strategy must not lose sight is the need to put the customer and/or employee at the center of everything it does. And the best way to frame that discussion is to begin by agreeing to give them what they want.

Giving Users What They Want

Chamillionaire is a Grammy and MTV Music Award–winning hip-hop artist and producer with multiple Top Ten and Platinum records to his name. He has also emerged as one of the industry's most tech-savvy CEOs. Giving his stakeholders, a.k.a. his *fans*, what they want was no small task in the world of major label entertainment, but Chamillionaire wasn't deterred by the challenge. He developed *Chamillitary*—a unique gamified approach to community building online that has become a model for how to engage fickle stakeholders and drive the behavior of an entire fan base (Figure 2.2).

While much had been made of engaging music fans on social media, Cham (as his most loyal fans call him) wanted to do something more powerful. A fan's energy can be a powerful thing as most of us have experienced at one point or another while listening to or watching the work of a performer we admire. After seeing the lengths to which his fans will go in order to build connections to his music and his persona, Cham decided on a simple philosophy:

FIGURE 2.2 Grammy-award winning artist and entrepreneur Chamillion-aire uses his fan website to drive engagement with gamification, where top fans can exchange points for prizes.

"Give the customers what they want... as long as they do something for me." That same approach works surprisingly well for all customer-centric organizations.

Chamillitary sets one basic goal: compete to be Chamillionaire's biggest fan. By accepting challenges and promoting newly released content, users earn points to be redeemed for special events and merchandise, as well as bragging rights. While there are many unorthodox elements in the *Chamillitary* approach—for example, the opportunity to win a personalized outgoing voice mail message—the fundamental conceit sounds fairly straightforward and conservative. Though you can win eccentric prizes including one of Cham's previously worn tank tops or a signed gold record, the basic model is "earn and burn"—just like most loyalty programs based on earning points and redeeming them for merchandise or services.

But unlike any other loyalty program around, you see how fundamentally the rules of engagement have been rewritten between Chamillionaire's thousands of fans and the artist they love. Through this new approach, he has been able to seed the market with new music and push it onto key charts without the weight of a major record label. He releases new merchandise and distributes it virally, growing his fan base through challenges designed to maximize reach, such as those designed to get groups together for listening parties. The *Chamillitary* system is even designed in such a way that new fans—those perhaps discovering Cham's music for the first time—travel through a special onboarding process. This *first-time experience* is designed to train new users on how the *Chamillitary* works, expose them to new music, and create a sense of immediate progress, rich with positive reinforcement.

Rather than leave his music's discovery to chance or to the vagaries of the iTunes store, all of this is in the control of the artist and his fans. Gamification has changed their dialogue. In fact, it has *created* a dialogue. During his 2012 Gamification Summit keynote address, Chamillionaire recalled an interaction with a fan: "I went to the gym to work out," he explained. "A guy stopped me and said, 'I'm your biggest fan. When's your next mixtape dropping?' I turned to him and said, 'Wait a minute. I just dropped a mixtape. What's your position on the leaderboard?'" The fan didn't have an answer. "'You don't know?'" Chamillionaire asked him dubiously before retorting, "'You're definitely not my biggest fan.'"

The question of who is Chamillionaire's biggest fan can now be answered quantifiably, thanks to *Chamillitary*. And the basic premise of the game is simple: give people what they want, to get what you want, and vice versa. Gone are the days of simply producing great music and movies (or products, art, or anything else) and simply expecting fans to be there. As the average half-life of consumer engagement has fallen, so too have the walls that divide celebrity from layperson. Fans are willing to pay (with money and time) to connect with their favorite content creators, and the key is to make that possible, and obviously fun. But first, you have to see engagement as important before you can define it as a priority.

GAMIFY YOUR READ

Answer in one word: Chamillionaire uses his game *Chamillitary* to harness the energy of his, what?

Making Engagement the Number One Job

Nextjump understands the need to make engagement a key objective. The company's founder, Charlie Kim, took over 15 years to build Nextjump, an employee incentive provider, into one of the powerhouses of that cutthroat industry. Along the way, the organization has developed a corporate culture that is the envy of most of its competitors. The company is a glowing example of a practice-what-you-preach community.

From its extraordinary achievements in employee health and wellness (detailed more closely in Chapters 6 and 7) to its unusually low turnover and high employee satisfaction, Nextjump has distinguished itself as a leader in employee drive and engagement. Kim, the company's CEO, credits the company's focus on overall employee connectedness with the company's longevity and financial success. By gamifying everything including training tactics to tying games to employee bonuses, Nextjump has made fun a priority.

Engagement was also job number one when the U.S. Army decided to develop *America's Army* (AA)—a game based around the experience of a soldier (also further detailed in Chapter 6). The project, which replaced dozens of failed attempts to build a military simulation game that would be played by the masses, went on to become one of the most popular games of all time.

The stroke of genius driving *America's Army* came from retired colonel Casey Wardynski, the economist-turned-gamification expert behind the project. Instead of simply trying to educate prospective soldiers on the possibilities of a career in the armed forces, *America's Army* let them experience it. The game allowed people to reenact the experience of a soldier, rather than simply filling out a meaningless recruitment questionnaire. It's not that questionnaires are bad, per se. It's just that they could be so much better.

If the U.S. Army appears to understand the power of engagement as a predictor of success, Nextjump's Kim sees it even more succinctly. According to him, your gamification strategy needs to "begin with employees, then extend to customers." Kim believes that by starting with internal stakeholders, you can prove the value of your approach before releasing it to the world and reap its benefits for your organization. This approach has served the company well, helping it to launch breakthrough gamified products that started out as employee-facing projects. This includes oo.com—Nextjump's social giving platform driven by gamification. The site makes it possible for users to amplify their charitable giving by shopping with merchants that offer charity rewards for loyalty. After employees successfully proved that people would shop incrementally more with a social mission in mind (when it was fun), the company made it into a product.

Knowing When the Game Is the Thing

The interplay between using a gamified experience as a tactic that supports your core business or *as a business in and of itself* is central to correctly utilizing games. Companies that are able to recognize when the game has become popular enough to stand on its own must be able to respond quickly and open up new lines of business, service, and revenue opportunities as a result. Simultaneously, companies wrestling with the fear that a game will overwhelm their core product must watch carefully in order to avoid the realization of those fears.

Obviously, U.S. airlines like United and American understand this lesson clearly. From 2002 to 2006, the domestic airline industry collectively lost close to $20 billion on flying customers around. Meanwhile, their loyalty programs remained in the black. These frequent-flier programs are in fact gamified strategies to raise engagement and generate incremental revenue. In the case of these two airlines, their game overwhelmed the core offering (flying planes) in terms of profitability, consistency, and consumer satisfaction. Is that necessarily a bad thing?

Consider the value of these frequent-flier economies: in 2009, American Airlines' AAdvantage program issued 175 billion frequent-flier miles. Of these, two-thirds were to third-party issuers, including financial institutions, merchants, and other loyalty operators, who paid American for every mile they gave out as a reward. The numbers are powerful: every mile issued by a credit card company represents money the bank is earning in merchant, financing, and miscellaneous fees associated with consumer charging activity. So deeply are these businesses enmeshed that during the extensive airline bankruptcies of 2010, the biggest bailouts came from their loyalty card issuing banks. Without the opportunity for those points, customers wouldn't charge as much on their cards, and the banks stood to lose billions. From the perspective of companies like Chase, United Airlines actually *is* too big to fail.

So if we look critically at the airlines of today, we should ask a question: what business are they in, exactly? Running an airline with a loyalty program, or running a loyalty program that happens to have an airline? When does the *game become the thing*?

This isn't a question that plagues online question-and-answer (Q&A) leader StackOverflow. This unique community has accomplished something most people wouldn't think possible: it has marshaled over a million leading software developers and experts to help each other out completely for free. Unlike other Q&A sites, including the much-maligned Yahoo! Answers, the on-demand ChaCha, and the hyped Quora, StackOverflow's community is extraordinarily qualified and dedicated.

Every day, thousands of individuals—most of whom charge hundreds of dollars per hour for their professional consulting services in the real world—help answer each other's questions on

StackOverflow. The difference is that on StackOverflow they do it for free. They compile code, write subroutines, form ad hoc groups, and do intense research, all to solve each other's problems. Their reward: a "virtual currency" called *reputation points* and the occasional badge—both symbols of their status within the community. No cash changes hands among users. In fact, everything that happens on the site is about establishing credibility, gaining bragging rights, and helping others. The reputation points are earned for various activities like commenting or voting for or against the comments of other users, and they are balanced in favor of quality over quantity—making it quite difficult to spam the service. These gamified dynamics enable the company to deliver top-flight technical support without labor costs. We discuss the dynamics of StackOverflow's success in greater detail in Chapter 10.

So successful was StackOverflow itself (just ask any techie you know) that the company pivoted its business model and became StackExchange. This new approach reprises the successful design of StackOverflow for other companies, delivering vertical communities based on the same premise of gamified support and sharing. Today, dozens of companies rely on this concept for crowdsourced support—all without any money changing hands at the end user level. StackExchange understood that the game was, ultimately, the product. It realized it could use the game to drive its overall strategic innovation, creating a unique center of excellence and revenue stream within the organization.

Creating a Center of Excellence and Innovation

Success with gamification has driven smaller organizations to create products and pivot strategies to account for changing markets and opportunities. But larger organizations haven't stayed out of the game, recognizing that success with gamification techniques can help create *centers of excellence* that drive employee, product, and customer behavior beyond traditional methods. These internal groups largely become resources for the entire organization, helping the company reach new heights.

One of the least likely leaders of this movement is SAP—the German enterprise software giant. Founded in 1972, this $75 billion company is the leader in enterprise software, driving the back end for most of the world's largest companies. The image the company projects is as staid, dependable, and congenial German engineers, which is reinforced by both the company's branding ("The best companies run on SAP") and its conservative, refined software.

But under the covers, SAP is leading a revolution in enterprise gamification. Since 2008, it has been using its techniques across a wide range of functions, most notably as part of the SAP community network. This online system is designed to connect SAP corporate clients across the world in order to solicit feedback, share information, and disseminate the best practices about SAP's complex software and technology road map. Today, over 30,000 people use the system on a regular basis—which is a sizable chunk of the target market—and gamification is at the heart of this engagement economy. Customers can earn points, badges, and achievements in line with knowledge and sharing to bring the company incalculable brand, feature, and support innovations.

But it was what SAP did with its results that was truly amazing. Starting as a small gamification project to enhance the external community, Mario Herger, leader of the initiative internally, began to drive gamification into other areas of the company, including SAP's notable *Innovation Days*. Throughout the year, teams from across the organization come together to compete in an effort to deliver new features and subproducts to customers. Over the last

GAMIFY YOUR READ

Answer in one word: The SAP community network is designed to connect whom?

Selling Gamification as a Strategy

As any seasoned corporate warrior will tell you, half the battle is setting expectations the right way from the get-go. Are we raising engagement or generating revenue? Is this to beat the competition or to change the game entirely? Check out http://gamrev.com for some brilliant insights from SAP's Mario Herger on how to get the organization behind your gamification strategy.

few cycles, these events have focused on gamification. As a result, teams have brought gamified design to mundane, core software modules—like data entry. The teams' imagination has yielded numerous trophies, helping the company make even the most boring interactions more dynamic and engaging. The ideas the teams generate are being spread throughout the organization, with SAP product and strategy teams incorporating engagement and fun into the business repertoire.

SAP is using these approaches to change its internal systems and engage its professional community, while at the same time investing to spin the ideas out and commoditize them to customers. An emphasis on creating a center of excellence around gamification has yielded products and services that generate new revenue streams, attract new customers, drive innovation, and lower the cost of talent acquisition. This of course makes gamification more sustainable by attaching it to a direct revenue stream. But it also demonstrates that gamification can do more than raise "soft" measures like engagement. It can make money.

IBM, the vaunted software and services company, has taken it a step further. As part of an internal project, the company built the *Smart Play Framework*—a platform to help make gamification easier and more scalable in the enterprise. Using its own internally developed approach, IBM has launched more than 9 unique products externally, and 50 internally, including these:

➤ *Innov8.* A simulation system designed to spur companywide innovation

➤ *CityOne.* A simulation game that addresses real-life urban issues such as water purification

➤ *SimArchitect.* A gamified design experience that renders cutting-edge design without the real-world costs

What the company has accomplished is impressive both in its scale and its impact. Today, thousands of organizations use IBM's spun-out games to learn, simulate scenarios, and build their own strategies for dealing with an uncertain future (some of which are explored more closely in Chapter 10). The company's expertise in strategic gamification sets it apart and helps drive both sales and, ultimately, revenue. Today, IBM's top global lead generator is its business process management (BPM) game *Innov8*. To wit, this gamified experience was instrumental in helping the company launch its global BPM practice in 2011.

Beyond this, the company has excelled at gamifying the interaction between team members as well. Using the *IBM Learning Commons* (a gamified education platform) as a training tool and *WebAlive* (a gamelike chat system) to develop communication, tens of thousands of IBMers have been trained at a fraction of the cost—and with increased efficacy—compared to traditional methods. Each one of these products has been made available to customers or has been considered as an external product.

The extent to which IBM and other companies have capitalized on gamification is astounding, but ultimately they're all taking a page from the strategies of Nextjump's Kim: experiment internally, and then turn that gamification into a product or experience for customers.

———

Whether it's a services and tech behemoth like IBM, an arm of the government like the U.S. military, or a fan community built around a charismatic artist like Chamillionaire, there are key strategic patterns that recur. Understanding the importance of engagement, giving users what they want, orienting around the user, hiring a chief engagement officer, and embracing the game as it grows are all leading-edge gamification strategies that top companies have employed. This trend will only continue as gamification demonstrates its unique power to drive scalable results.

In parallel, some organizations are using gamification along with strategy in a completely different way. In addition to making gamification a core part of their strategy, they are using it to make strategic processes themselves more engaging. By bringing these techniques to strategic development approaches, they are raising the participation of stakeholders, driving unique outcomes, and reimagining strengths, weaknesses, opportunities, and threats (SWOT) analyses in new and much more exciting ways.

3

GAMIFYING THE STRATEGIC PROCESS

In 1994 three pioneers in game theory were awarded the Nobel Prize. John Nash, Richard Selton, and John Harsanyl had each developed and refined groundbreaking mathematical theories around economics and games. In particular, they achieved notoriety for their work on *noncooperative interactions*—or those in which binding agreements between parties are not possible. Chess,

GAMIFY YOUR READ

Riddle Me This!

Read the chapter for clues to answer the following riddle: What atmospheric condition uses thunder, lightning, and heavy rains in formulating fun?

To see if your answer is correct, unlock a range of bonus content, and engage with fellow readers, visit *The Gamification Revolution* app, which can be downloaded at http://gamrev.com! You may also verify your answer by visiting the answer key at the back of the book.

checkers, poker, and other games of strategy served as the foundation for their work in this powerful field of game theory—now regarded as the most prevalent system for analyzing strategic decision making. Only two other game theorists had ever won before, but afterward, the floodgates opened. Game theorists subsequently won the award over the next two years with five additional winners in the last decade alone.

Game theory is "the study of mathematical models of conflict and cooperation between rational decision makers." In other words, it uses the *system of games* to model potential end results. Although game theory should not be confused with game design (or even gamification design), they have a similar history of meeting initial resistance in corporate America. Game theory was first described as early as the eighteenth century, but it began its corporate ascent through work at the famous analysis firm, the RAND Corporation, in the postwar era. Today, it's used by a plurality of the world's major companies and governments.

Game theory is fundamentally flawed in its emphasis on "rational decision making." After all, how often are decisions made rationally rather than emotionally? And what percentage of the time do people even utilize deliberate decision-making criteria versus acting on reflex or instinct? In the bestselling books *Blink* (Malcolm Gladwell) and *Nudge* (Richard Thaler and Cass Sunstein), the authors make the compelling case that we often act irrationally and with significant mental biases.

This shouldn't be taken as an indictment of game theory. Rather, it is an opportunity to contextualize its appropriate use: as a powerful tool in the corporate strategy framework, enhanced by a broader, more emotional view of our customers and employees. Perhaps if we take a broader view—one that looks at both the math and the emotions behind decision making—we can build a stronger strategic process. This in turn should leave our organizations better prepared for the future.

Therein lies the promise of the gamification of strategy—by using the key strengths of gamification, the strategic process gets better, which in turn improves outcomes. The gamification of strategy promises such opportunities as these:

> Understanding the end game
> Modeling scenarios
> Creating engagement
> Raising intelligence

Let's take a closer look at how gamification can be employed in these areas to improve strategic processes and outcomes.

Understanding the End Game

One of the reasons many executives are attracted to gamification in strategy is a fairly well understood bias. In business, as in games, we play to win—though *winning* often means different things in different contexts. Sometimes, there are short-term losses to secure long-term gains. And, most critically, we need to be able to think multiple steps ahead, anticipate what will come next, and prepare for it.

The definition of the term *end game* constitutes one major difference between business and game strategy. While most classic games do eventually reach a finite end—even if from attrition—most organizations plan as though there were no end. The key is to find a strategically gamified approach that can deliver the right time horizon for the planning process without expecting players to stay engaged beyond a reasonable limit.

One great example of this was the *alternate reality game* (ARG) *World Without Oil*, developed in 2007 by Ken Eklund and Jane McGonigal for PBS's *Independent Lens*. *World Without Oil* asked participants to imagine themselves in various roles in the aftermath of a major oil shock. Over 32 days (simulating 32 weeks), 1,800 participants (and 60,000 observers) helped shape what the United States might look like without oil. At its worst, gas hit $7 a gallon, 2 million people lost their jobs, cities suffered over $1 billion in damages from rioting and civil disorder, and vast numbers of people were displaced and living in Federal Emergency Management Agency (FEMA) camps, or migrating across the country looking for jobs. (See Figure 3.1.)

World Without Oil didn't reach a finite conclusion—identifying exactly what would happen to a country without a key energy supply. It didn't seek to model the specific price of gas or number of dead, or the exact toll in suffering. What it did was lay out a rich trove of content (in the form of text, video, audio, and art). By playing with an open population and for a limited time, this ARG provided invaluable insights about how people might react to such a crisis. For organizations, this type of gamified approach to strategy formulating can provide a view of the "human side" and serve as a powerful enhancement to the statistical results generated by other modeling approaches.

World Without Oil asked a specific if open-ended question: What would a future look like without black gold? The same premise can be used for any business's strategic process as well. Whether looking to figure out pricing, identifying competition, or seeking a merger partner, companies are almost always asking: *What will*

FIGURE 3.1 *World Without Oil* gave players the chance to imagine the United States in the middle of oil crises for which the players were asked to seek solutions.

Did you know the word *strategy* itself comes from the Greek word *strategia* meaning "office of the general" or "generalship"? Is it surprising that the language of war is as popular in the boardroom as it is on the battlefield?

We've long known that the great chess players are great strategists, so it should come as no surprise that some of the best CEOs of our time have also been master chess players. *Business Insider* compiled a list of executives with chess pedigrees, and the list included champions Duncan Suttles, president of Magnetar Games, and Victoria Livschitz, founder and CEO of Grid Dynamics.

happen in the future? Just as chess players work backward from checkmate to their next move, strategic gamification helps drive novel solutions to significant future problems.

Interestingly, gamifying strategy works for both open-ended as well as *specific* future questions. While classic game theory approaches, emphasizing numerical outcomes and large-scale micro-decision modeling, probably work best for specific questions, softer gamified approaches—such as *World Without Oil*—can help fill in the other side of the equation—the human side. Taken together, they can help us form a clearer picture of the future.

What some of the world's most successful strategic planners possess is the ability to design, execute, and understand the results of scenario models. This skill can be leveraged and improved in powerful ways through gamification—and it is already becoming a core strength among leading organizations around the world.

Modeling Scenarios: The Simulation Game as a Crystal Ball

Scenario planning has been a mainstay of corporate strategy approaches since its advent in the 1950s at the RAND Corporation. Originally developed as a way of thinking through geopolitical threats and opportunities, scenario planning today is being used to imagine all aspects of a complex future—and not just in the political sphere. Today's scenario planning in all its incarnations focuses on using stories (scenarios) to drive a reaction from a human or computer subject. These reactions are then compiled, synthesized, and used to drive change or preparedness now and in the future.

By the 1980s, over 50 percent of Fortune 500 companies were using scenario modeling, and that number has only grown. Energy giant Royal Dutch Shell is among the technique's chief proponents. The company describes scenario planning this way: "Carefully crafted stories about the future embodying a wide range of ideas [usefully] integrated." The company maintains that building scenarios helps people link an uncertain future with the decisions of today.

Business-is-war (BIW) *games* are the most familiar kind of gamified scenario-based strategy tools. BIW games generally include simulations and exercises that allow individuals to move step-by-step through an experience using a game environment to help assess potential outcomes.

Negotiation-based games are among the most popular in the BIW category. Generally, they are designed as simulations that allow executives to play both sides of a scenario and negotiate as opposing parties. The newest approaches incorporate competitive intelligence and shifting environmental data to ensure that the negotiator is prepared for real-world success. As a sign of its popu-

Shell Scenarios and *World Without Oil*

Shell uses scenarios both as an internal planning tool and as a part of its global communication strategy. You can see and interact with a subset of its energy future scenarios, and you can explore the results of strategy games like *World Without Oil* at the social app for *The Gamification Revolution* by downloading it at http://gamrev.com.

larity, every U.S. Army officer since 2007 has undergone negotiation game–based training before gaining authorization to interact with civilian populations.

Despite the military's support, scenario-based strategy (and training) has remained somewhat controversial because of the lack of demonstrable proof that it can accurately predict the future. All the same, the techniques are extraordinarily popular—gaining renewed momentum when the collapse of Lehman Brothers in 2008 was anticipated by bond company PIMCO in one of their scenarios. Other, more quantitative models failed to see the impending collapse, but PIMCO's use of scenarios revealed the human side of the model and led to the seemingly clairvoyant catch.

Research on the use of formal game concepts in scenario planning isn't exactly new. With the publication of the *Management Science* article "A Competitive Scenario Modeling System" in 1980 (Biplab Dutta and William King), scientists and process experts began looking at the use of gamification for scenarios. Competition, teams, leaderboards, points, judging, and prizing are all mechanics described in the literature as approaches used to enhance planning. Companies as diverse as Apple and AutoNation have used advanced gamified scenarios to look at major market shifts—from chip pricing and availability to consumer preferences, respectively—and their impact on each company's future.

Rigorous analysis of the efficacy of gamified strategy planning—even compared to nongamified scenarios—tends to yield ambiguous results. Both Dutta and King's research and the Murray Turoff–led 2005 landmark work *Scenario Development Gaming* show that people prefer a gamified approach to traditional methods (pen and paper, lectures, and so on). While this shouldn't be shocking—who wouldn't rather play a game than sit in a chair and write all day?—the tangible benefits have not been easy to identify.

Participants who have used gamified strategic planning methods have expressed that increased information was the main benefit they got out of it, as compared to the older approaches. The other observed benefit was that the gamified approaches tended to more readily challenge players' underlying assumptions by forcing them to hone in on the specifics of a situational narrative from, in some cases, an alternative perspective. This is an incredibly important capability when a process relies on internal stakeholders— especially since biases can be difficult to spot.

The heuristic benefits of gamified scenario planning alone are likely strong enough to motivate most organizations to adopt the approach. Today, however, organizations using gamified planning are demonstrating its value in even more tangible ways.

WikiStrat is a U.S. and Israeli start-up billing itself as the world's first "massively multiplayer online consultancy." The founders' concept was to bring the power of gamification to strategic process and analysis, with an emphasis on geopolitical strategies and war games.

The way WikiStrat works is that each project is treated as a competition, where a global network of vetted analysts and subject matter experts create scenarios in response to a client's input. Such projects can take very broad and abstract forms (for example, "What will Russia's global influence look like in 2050?") or very specific ones (for example, "What effect would ethnic strife in China have on the semiconductor industry?"). In every case, these analysts—most of whom are scattered around the world—develop scenarios based on their expertise and submit them to the WikiStrat community (as well as the interested client). Based on votes and feedback, the best scenario wins, and the top analyst gets paid.

According to Daniel Green, WikiStrat's cofounder, the company delivers projects in a more scalable and cost-effective fashion than its competitors. Because many of its analysts work for other organizations in similar capacities as well, WikiStrat takes advantage of its expertise at a lower hourly cost. It is therefore imperative that WikiStrat create engagement with its analysts.

Green says the company has found through analysis that its contributors report consistently that this "side job" is more fun than their day job. It's the component of fun building additional engagement that has helped the fledgling company sign significant scenario analysis deals with major governments and Fortune 100s, snatching contracts from established firms around the world. Additionally, the gamification elements have proven particularly powerful at winning over skeptics.

Green recounted the story of a senior agent, let's call him B. B was in his fifties, had a long and distinguished career in government intelligence, and had started working for Wikistrat on the side. His dislike of the gamification elements was immediate, and he told the founders that he would overlook the points and levels, which he found childish. Within weeks, B had become among the most vocal supporters of the system, e-mailing almost daily to find out how to raise his ranking, challenging others to outdo him, and greatly improving his performance. Wikistrat's well-designed gamified solution tapped into B's desire for mastery and latent competitiveness, triggering exactly the right response: better, faster, and cheaper strategic analysis.

Another organization that's seen the benefits of gamified scenario planning is Fuld & Company—one of the world's leading competitive intelligence consultancies. It has run *Fuld War Game Battles* for over six years, pitting the best MBA students from top schools against each other to assess outcomes for various challenges. Past battles have focused on topics as diverse as the future of food, China's electrical grid, and mobile telephony, bringing together students from Northwestern, Yale, Harvard, MIT, and Dartmouth.

In the case of the 2011 *Battle for Designer Foods*, Abbot, Danone, GlaxoSmithKline, and Nestlé were stress tested to see how they would position their brands to appeal to an emerging $20 billion consumer market. Teams were tasked with developing strategies that would yield maximum revenues in a three-year period based on suggested figures and specific scenario variables.

Over the years, the competition has proven itself to be surprisingly accurate in predicting some "unpredictable" outcomes. For example, previous battles anticipated Google's advertising dominance as well as Apple's foray into TV and social networking. Of course, they have been wrong as often as they've been right—

but between the economic value and the wealth of collected data from the challenges, Fuld, the students, and companies involved are doing the impossible: they are telling the future.

The use of gamification in scenario-building techniques across the wide range of examples highlighted here can help improve the accuracy of predicted outcomes and reduce the cost of their ultimate delivery. Whether using internal stakeholders or external organizations to do the work, businesses can tap into a vast reserve of intellectual capital using game-based approaches. Regardless of which community you tap into or which tack you take, ensuring expert engagement in the problems of today will be critical to the success of your business tomorrow and every day thereafter.

Creating Engagement

Engagement matters because it predicts superior outcomes. Experts at the Futures Strategy Group (FSG) have summarized the value of games and gamification to that end in their *FSG Outlook* analysis of scenarios, explaining, "Games bring the competitive landscape to life." The more real a scenario feels to the users, the better it will run.

This need to bring engagement to scenario planning and analysis was at the forefront of Adobe's mind when the company convened over 40 team members to a strategy planning session in 2011. Like most strategy events, participants were eager to get involved for the good of the company (and a day out of the routine), but the challenges of a frenetic workplace were never far from the room. Despite everyone's best efforts, important e-mails, phone calls, crises, and other interruptions prevented the audience members from staying fully engaged throughout the process. However, through the use of gamification techniques like *gamestorming* (a combination of games and brainstorming), over 90 percent of the team members joined in the program and stayed until the end.

But keeping people in the room isn't the only metric for defining engagement. Rather, creating and sustaining active participation

Native American Talking Sticks

The Native American talking stick was a tool used by some aboriginal tribes worldwide to ensure democracy during meetings. In modern use, the object need not necessarily be a literal stick; however, the concept remains the same: the holder of the talking stick gets to speak.

The talking stick has been used to ensure that everyone who wants to speak is heard, so that some voices don't dominate the discussion. In a similar fashion, many gamestorming tools are designed to ensure a more democratic view of creativity and expression in the workplace—allowing quieter voices to be heard. Learn more about gamestorming by visiting *The Gamification Revolution* app. Access it now at http://gamrev.com.

is key. Gamestorming does just that. By replacing standard business meetings and brainstorming techniques with more gamified approaches, interests are piqued and people are compelled to see their ideas through from beginning to end. While gamestorming concepts go back for centuries (Native American talking sticks are one example of a communication technique that inspires current designers), in the modern era they are uniquely rooted in the language of contemporary games and business culture.

One of the features that distinguishes gamestorming is its focus on the overall narrative of the experience—in other words, sessions begin by establishing and defining rules. At the end of game play, the game world is closed with some meaningful resolution. This approach allows players to suspend disbelief and take themselves out of the everyday to focus on the activity at hand.

Gamestorming in Practice

Many gamestorming games take typical strategy processes like analyzing revenue and present them as a game using mechanics such as points and rewards to inspire momentum. The game *3-12-2*, for example, adapted from the book *Gamestorming* (Dave Gray, Sunni Brown, and James Macanufo) uses constraints, focused tasks, forced rankings, and closures to drive intense idea creation within a short period of time.

The game begins by posing an open-ended question to the group, like this one: How do we increase revenue in the next five years? Working individually, for the first 3 minutes players write down on individual index cards, rather than *answers* to the proposed conundrum, *aspects* of the problem. Typically, this is done in simple statements (nouns and verbs), and players are encouraged to write down as many as they can.

Aspects of the problem might include these:

➤ Economy is unstable.
➤ Key customers are retiring.
➤ Product development cycle is aging.

Accurate timekeeping is essential, and after 3 minutes are over, cards are shuffled.

Players are put into teams of two, and for the next 12 minutes, they draw cards from the pile to use as inspiration toward solving the problem. They are not constrained by the aspect they draw from the pile, but the aspect should be used as a trigger point for problem solving. While they may ideate as many concepts as they want, ultimately they should work toward one great idea (and you'd be well served to tell them so).

After 12 minutes are up, the pairs shift into groups of six to eight. Each pair then gets 2 minutes to pitch their best idea. The groups use their remaining 2 minutes to decide on the best idea to share with the collective. Each team may offer one or more ideas to the larger group based on the total number of people involved in the process. The game is best if the finished experience yields at least 10 good ideas.

Every top idea should be written out in front of the group after which, everyone may vote on a favorite. The total number of votes per individual is equal to the number of ideas his or her team presented **plus one**. This plus one ensures that even if they decide to vote based on partisanship (instead of on merit), they must still choose one more idea that would win on merit.

Once the results are in, the scores are tallied and a winner is declared. In this way, the game world is closed and resolution is achieved. This sense of closure is especially important for competitive people, but all players will appreciate it. You'll notice that the game does not close by promising an implementation of the ideas. Rather, a different goal or objective is created: in this case, one or several game-winning ideas. By focusing on idea generation and ranking, we know that we can always achieve the goal of the game, regardless of quality. Therefore, players feel that their time spent was worthwhile, and we build trust. Further, by strictly enforcing a time limit, players are also helped to focus and to feel relief when the game is complete.

Games like *3-12-2* are extraordinarily powerful at generating ideas. In one experiment at a GSummitX meetup in Boston, a room of 80 strangers dove deeply into the engagement issues of the Boston Museum of Science. The museum, one of the leading public facilities of its kind, sought to increase adult attendance and to grow its membership base. In the 45 minutes it took to play the game, attendees ideated hundreds of solutions. Winners were given nominal schwag as prizes, but no other compensation was offered. The game successfully triggered the players' desire to contribute, the time limits made it feel achievable, and the rules as well as the subsequent cooperation made it fun.

This gamestorming pattern has been repeated dozens of times in organizations throughout the world. Whether the groups consist of people who are already teamed up at work or they consist of unaffiliated individuals brought into a room together for this one purpose, there is no equivalent for the power of gamification to drive engagement in the context of strategy. The upshot is increased productivity, satisfaction, and, ultimately, quality.

Raising Intelligence

One overlooked way to increase the quality of strategic analysis inside an organization might seem farfetched at first. However, raising the intelligence quotient of those engaged in defining strategy is actually a viable solution—that is, if games are used to make people *smarter.*

"Of course," you say (maybe while rolling your eyes). "Who wouldn't want to snap a couple of fingers and make their team smarter?" Most companies believe that the only way to maximize intelligence within their teams is to hire for it at the outset. After all, if you recruit the smartest, most motivated, best-interacting people in the world, you will logically achieve the best possible results. If intelligence were fixed and immutable as so many people believe, you would be right.

However, research now shows that **we can actively raise intelligence**—particularly the two kinds of intelligence that matter most to strategic planning: *emotional intelligence*—commonly known as EI or EQ—and *fluid intelligence*—abbreviated Gf, G being the scientific notation for intelligence.

Emotional intelligence refers to the ability to leverage the right emotional state for a given situation. It is largely considered a key predictor of success. Numerous studies, including a fascinating look at EI in hardcore sports by the Peak Performance Institute, have found that people with higher EI generally perform better at challenges than others. The basic premise asserts that if you understand and channel the right emotional energy for the right situation, your kinesthetic performance will improve.

Fluid intelligence refers to the ability to solve problems and reason clearly in novel situations, particularly when there is no direct knowledge from which to draw. This is different from general *crystallized intelligence* (Gc), which refers to the ability to use existing skills or knowledge. Crystallized intelligence is the ability that is commonly evaluated in standardized tests—including most corporate recruitment tests.

Clearly, in strategic planning situations, both EI and Gf come in handy. EI ensures the team members can challenge each other without descending into histrionics. At the core of EI is an ability to understand appropriate emotional responses as well as an inclination toward empathy. Gf lets team members bring maximum problem-solving skills to the table along with speed and mental agility. It goes without saying that an ideal strategy team would be made up of members with the right levels of both. Whether the right results are derived in real-world or virtual scenarios can be highly dependent on whether the team members have high EI and Gf abilities. So what if people aren't scoring as high as they should? Or what if high scorers could score even higher?

Barbara Kerr, workplace development expert, is the creator of one of the world's first games targeted at raising EI. *Creating an Emotionally Intelligent World* is a game designed to help corporate teams increase their EI scores through a series of role-playing activities modeled around real-world scenarios. Kerr's 12 years of experience working on EI issues in corporations led her to develop the game as an improved method of training. The game, described as "fast-paced, thought-provoking and fun," was developed after Kerr realized that traditional means of delivery including lectures and pamphlets weren't getting her point across.

"It didn't take me long to understand," she says, "that a detailed PowerPoint presentation was not an effective means for conveying either the concepts or my own enthusiasm for the possibilities of enhancing emotional intelligence."

Kerr's game was an outgrowth of her professional development practice, and it uses time—instead of money—as the principal currency (that is, the better you do, the more free time you get). As you progress through the experience, you can land on "challenge" or "opportunity" squares that allow you to take actions based on your level of EI. Additionally, you can find yourself on an "unexpected life event" (ULE) square that forces you to deal with exceptionally challenging situations (like the death of a loved one or the loss of a job) based not on your own EI level but on the EI level to which you've been assigned during play. The game's long arc is to show how people with different levels of EI might respond differently to various situations—helping them manage others and develop their own skills in the process.

Creating an Emotionally Intelligent World isn't the only product on the market. Franklin Learning of Connecticut also publishes *EQ for Success* (for corporations) and the *Emotional Intelligence Game* (for children). At the same time, customized solutions are also continuing to appear. In one powerful case study, gamified modalities were used to raise EI among U.S. Marines. In an intercultural role-playing game, the idea was to generate self-awareness through "crucible" experiences in which players were forced to actually grow as people. A stress-centric design like that might be difficult to imagine in the average workplace, but if it has produced increased emotional intelligence for Marines, it could certainly be adapted for use in a corporate setting.

With increased EI comes better interactions and better group decision making. With increased Gf, organizations can take advantage of significantly enhance intellectual power to better solve strategic problems. Solutions like *N-Back*—a game that recently vaulted into the public consciousness—do just that.

The concept behind *n*-back games is relatively straightforward. Players are presented with a sequence of letters and a variable (n) that represents a number. Their goal is to remember the letters as they stream by and indicate when one is offered that corresponds to a matching item from n back.

For example, where n is 3, you're given a stream of letters like these (read from left to right):

L H M F H E Z R Z X R

The boldfaced letters *H* and *R* would be called out because they represent the letters given 3 (n) letters ago. Similarly, you wouldn't call out any of the other letters because none of them were given 3 letters before. For example, there are 2 instances of the letter *Z*, but they are separated by only 1 other letter. Therefore, you wouldn't highlight the *Z* (as this particular game is about intervals of 3).

You can make the task harder by increasing *n* (it gets more challenging to remember what was previously said as the interval increases). In *Dual N-Back*, the game is made more complex by asking users to do this with two different kinds of inputs, like a letter and number or color and sound, simultaneously.

In multiple studies, *N-Back* and *Dual N-Back* raised fluid intelligence of participants by a significant amount—up to 5 IQ points in just four weeks of play. The halo effect of the game is also substantial, with results appearing stable after eight months or more. While some have reported 20-point result increases and more, others still question the efficacy of the experiments. One thing is certain: *N-Back* is having a major effect on our view of Gf and its stability. Perhaps getting smarter is as easy as playing a game?

It seems inevitable that future organizations will prescribe or encourage their employees to train with *n*-back games in the hope that they will increase Gf and—eventually—strategic outcomes. But with any such edict, the fun factor inevitably decreases when people are required to play it—another problem that might require another gamified solution! Because if organizations increase their strategic success by focusing on and developing both fluid and emotional intelligence, they will be primed for a strategic competitive advantage.

The gamification of strategy, with the right customization, is already driving excellence in today's leading companies. At its heart is a critical realization: organizations must obtain extraordinary results from their employees first and foremost. With gamification's strategic foundation in place, we can take the next step—engaging employees to deliver exceptional results.

GAMIFY YOUR READ

Riddle Me This!

Now that you've read the chapter and found the clues, answer the following riddle: What atmospheric condition uses thunder, lightning, and heavy rains in formulating fun?

To see if your answer is correct, unlock a range of bonus content, and engage with fellow readers, visit *The Gamification Revolution* app, which can be downloaded at http://gamrev.com! You may also verify your answer by visiting the answer key at the back of the book.

PART II

ENGAGING YOUR TEAM AND DRIVING RESULTS

4

SUPERCHARGING
STAFF PERFORMANCE

★

Today's employees are changing—and changing fast.
Surprisingly to most managers, over 50 percent of U.S. workers are dissatisfied with their jobs. Study after study shows a decline in satisfaction and engagement, which has been accelerated by the global financial crisis of 2008. Whether it's wages (only 35 percent satisfied), managerial quality (only 54 percent satisfied), or stress level (only 25 percent satisfied), a survey by Right Management, the talent and management subdivision of the staffing behemoth ManpowerGroup, shows an alarming level of worker disaffection. This trend has been accelerating since the late 1980s, with most indices declining at least 20 percent more since then.

As this news has filtered into the media, it's been rightly referred to as a "crisis." Given that 60 percent of the U.S. economy is service driven and that our future is dependent on high-impact knowledge work, employee motivation and drive must affect yield. Many politicians and business leaders, however, are content to ignore this risk. After all, if U.S. worker productivity continues to rise and unemployment remains stubbornly high, why does worker satisfaction matter?

But it is precisely for those reasons that satisfaction and engagement matter more than ever. Much of the United States' productivity gain over the last two decades has arisen from outsourcing everything possible, so the jobs that have remained are increasingly the only ones that can't be sent overseas. And while aggregate unemployment remains elevated, skilled workers—particularly in high-growth regions—continue to be in extraordinarily short supply. For example, the current unemployment rate for engineers in California's Silicon Valley is estimated to be less than 1 percent (compared to a 2012 national average well above 8 percent). While good for the engineers, it poses something of a challenge for those businesses hoping to retain the engineers that they have, while continuing to attract more.

Companies like Apple, which has generated a record $400,000 in profit per employee, also spend up to $125,000 when a skilled employee leaves—often losing up to 65 percent of productivity for a full year during the transition. And while high levels of unemployment have helped keep classic labor market unrest—like strikes and wage disputes—in check, knowledge workers at all ends of the economy aren't feeling pressure to stay in miserable working situations.

According to Right Management, fully 60 percent of surveyed workers are planning to change jobs as the economy improves. Even if this number is exaggerated by half, the effects on the global economy would be startling, and individual companies could be devastated.

This acute spike of disaffection is part of a larger trend toward reduced engagement and loyalty. No longer do people harbor the same cradle-to-grave work ethic of older generations. A Bureau of Labor Statistics (BLS) report from late 2010 brought forth the shocking realization that most active U.S. workers will have anywhere between 7 and 10 jobs in their lifetimes—with the potential for three or more distinct careers.

So if the fundamental, near-term prognosis for employee disengagement is so dire, it at least couldn't get any worse, right?

Wrong. The millennial generation, with over 150 million members in the United States and European Union alone, are just beginning to make their entrance. In so doing, they are bringing forward a unique worldview, shaped not only by their peers and their cultural milieu but also by the technologies with which they grew up.

As we are increasingly discovering, the specifics of their generational differences are jarring and already giving rise to significant management heartburn.

Managing this generation has become a hot button issue across industries. In fact, a Google search turns up nearly half a million results for "managing millennials," and the ranks of bestsellers on the subject is no slouch. Books such as *Keeping the Millennials*, *Managing the Millennials, Motivating the "What's in it for me" Generation,* and dozens of others demonstrate the intellectual currency of the question: Why are these brilliant, motivated, and technologically superliterate youngsters so hard to manage and optimize in the corporation?

The answer is disarmingly simple: games. Not just the games they played from their youngest years on their Nintendos, PlayStations, and home PCs but also the kinds of game mechanics at work in their lives. In his powerful book *Not Everyone Gets a Trophy*, Bruce Tulgan details a list of complaints about this generation he routinely hears from managers:

- ➤ "They walk in on day one with high expectations."
- ➤ "They don't want to pay their dues and climb the ladder."
- ➤ "It's hard to give them negative feedback without crushing their morale."
- ➤ "If you don't supervise them closely, they go off in the wrong direction."
- ➤ "They think everyone is going to give them a trophy just like they did growing up."

Research from consulting firm PricewaterhouseCoopers (PwC) amply backs this up. Millennials in the workforce said that 57 percent of them expect quick advancement. Furthermore, personal development was ranked their number one objective (ahead of remuneration). And, perhaps reflecting cynicism about the likelihood of having their needs met, 25 percent of them said they *expected* to have six or more employers in their lifetime. Optimism (or insouciance) of youth, perhaps—but a telling view nonetheless.

Tulgan's book title itself gives us the clue to the core issue that most nonmillennials have with this generation: that they are spoiled from having been given too much positive feedback or having won too many things in their life—the implication being, of course, that they got those things with less challenge or conflict than their predecessors.

While the symptoms are being correctly identified, we maintain that the cause is completely misunderstood. The millennial generation doesn't suffer from excessive positive reinforcement—those of us born before them simply *received too little.* In fact, the millennials are actually getting the amount of positive reinforcement most humans crave. They aren't receiving more trophies than they deserve, but rather their world offers more ways to earn trophies in the first place.

For this group, it is not getting the trophy itself that motivates them. It is that the lack of opportunity to win *demotivates* them. It is not that they don't want to pay their dues and climb the ladder. It is that they want there to be a discernible victory on every rung. They want to understand the rules for achieving that victory—and they have to believe they have a shot at winning it.

In most cases, the system doesn't yet exist whereby millennials can get what they want, leaving them disinterested and employers frustrated. But more and more often, businesses are making the requisite changes, and people are flocking to sign up for jobs that offer them. Amazon.com, Apple, and Google are ranked three of the top five companies where young people most want to work according to Universum, an employer branding firm. Perhaps not at all coincidentally, all three boast strong employee reward programs.

On the positive side, this generation is extraordinary at problem solving, organizing things out of chaos, multitasking, and being self-directed leaders—obviously key skills in the twenty-first-century global economy. Their view does not match that of preceding generations who, by and large, saw a strong work ethic as important in and of itself. In the past, incremental positive reinforcement might be looked on as unnecessary at best, or mollycoddling at worst. The core work values in our society said that you were supposed to do your best, delaying gratification and reward until the future.

The root cause of the glaring differences between the millennial generation and the rest of us is their inordinate exposure to games. When it comes to game play—whether online or off—this generation, unlike any before, has been exposed to continuous positive reinforcement. Additionally, they've been trained to view every challenge as a part of a progress system (like the levels within a game) with clearly articulated pathways. And, as in most games, they're expecting a ton of different ways to earn both real and proverbial trophies and achievements. Over time, and through this exposure, the millennial brain pathways have been altered, just as they would have been through any other kind of conditioning and reinforcement.

However, rather than raising philosophical questions about the nature of the millennial generation, we are better off raising those same questions about the nature of work itself. While we're at it, it can't hurt to look at our relationship to each other in the context of the workplace and consider what constitutes appropriate levels of feedback and reinforcement. While some of you might react with revulsion to these changed attitudes, rest assured that giving the millennial generation what they need to thrive doesn't require you to abandon your sense of propriety or hard work. On the contrary, it's about understanding how their approach to work is different and how gamification can help unlock their potential. The companies that have successfully been able to do this are able to crush their competition. After all, because of their game exposure, this generation is smarter, faster, more adaptable, more communicative, and more social than any other before.

In order to better achieve harmony with the new generation entering the workforce, let's first put the millennial management challenge in context. Much of what will drive their success in your organization will actually drive success throughout your employee community, no matter the generation. As you'll see below, the secrets of delivering maximum achievement in your organization are based on three primary drivers called the *three Fs: feedback, friends,* and *fun.* Organizations that can deliver those in the workplace can and will drive improved performance. What's more, these strategic drivers can be readily applied to every worker at your company whatever his or her age. While millennials might be driving this trend, all of us will benefit from it.

To understand how gamification can help raise employee engagement, satisfaction, performance, and tenure, we've organized Part II into function-based chapters. In the rest of this chapter, we'll look at how to set your team vision and goals in motion using gamification. Because every organization could be more innovative, Chapter 5 shares the strategies that winning companies have used to spark an innovation revolution in their ranks.

The Three *F*s: Feedback, Friends, and Fun

In analyzing a wide array of the best engagement experiences, a pattern starts to emerge: products and services that have generated the greatest amount of engagement and stickiness focus on *feedback, friends,* and *fun.* When present and authentic to the user in experiences, the resulting attraction and retention are the strongest. In brief:

Feedback is the act of telling users how they are progressing over time.

Friends are the connectors between users, whether they are friends in the classical sense or not.

Fun is fairly unique to each individual, but generally it is a sense of amusement or enjoyment.

When working together, these three drivers form the core of a viral engagement loop designed to propel users to visit an experience, return, and then also engage others to visit and return.

If your organization depends on proprietary bodies of knowledge to be successful, you'll find Chapter 6 on the gamification of recruitment and training to be critical to your future. So much innovation has been seen in this category that you might never think of posting a job ad or running a new employee seminar again.

Last, in Chapter 7 we'll look at employee health and wellness—a topic of growing concern in organizations and a goal that is as much about improving business outcomes as it is about lowering healthcare costs.

Ekins: Creating a Culture of Joy

In the 1970s Nike created a storytelling program designed as a one-hour introduction for new hires. The intention was to describe the experiences that led to the birth of the company—like how a running coach named Bill Bowerman helped to cofound the company after pouring rubber into his waffle maker in an attempt to make a better pair of running shoes for his runners (an exercise that ultimately gave the world Nike's famous "waffle soles").

In subsequent years the storytelling program has become a nine-day camp where Nike tech reps, who call themselves "Ekins" (which is *Nike* backward), literally live the history of the company: running the track where the company founders once trained and holding those rubber soles made by Bowerman's waffle iron. The program isn't centered around games, but it does utilize them to foster a sense of camaraderie among its staff members. At the end of the session, all of the participants are offered (and many agree to) a Nike swoosh tattoo on their leg.

Storytelling by itself isn't gamification; however, storytelling when married to gamification can be a powerful way to ally your employee base with your brand. The role of the Ekins is to proselytize for the brand. But more important, it is their job to *play its games and attract other people to play them too.* Today's Ekins are not only Nike's loudest advocates but they are also its frontline customers! The storytelling camp helps create meaning around

Up-or-Out Cultures

In many high-functioning organizations—consulting, for example—there seems to be a strong pressure for employees to move rapidly "up or out." The phrase suggests that personnel are encouraged to either rise quickly through the ranks or leave the company. The belief is that this kind of environment attracts highly motivated individuals in the first place and encourages the most competitive and driven to thrive. The concept seems at first blush to fit well with the millennial drive for continuous advancement, but it presents an immediate design challenge for a gamified system due to one basic reality: there are very few genuine advancement opportunities in most organizations. With few exceptions, only one person can become CEO, and anything that fundamentally tries to level that playing field may seem insincere.

For example, so-called flat organizations that de-emphasize moving up try to accomplish this by reducing the number of management layers. While this effort may be trying to convey a culture of egalitarianism, most achievement-oriented people will simply be turned off. After all, everyone knows the CEO still has the final say, despite there being fewer layers between the executive suite and the mailroom. At the same time, the opposite approach has its issues. Hardcore advancement-based strategies like "up or out" seem to be implicated in many ethical business failings. These include the Enron fiasco, in which the pressure to achieve in many cases trumped the individual's sense of right and wrong.

The right approach is to *create multiple tracks of significant meaning with disparate and clearly articulated levels.* This strategy allows employees to compete linearly on a specific track and/or to switch tracks and try out the experience in another area. While technology companies have long done this by encouraging employees to switch between technical and business tracks, the same thinking can be applied to any discipline. For example, in accounting, there can be

> strategy, forecasting, operations, treasury, and so on—and each can be interesting to different kinds of employees and at different times. The key is to define the tiers up front, create lots of interim steps, and give employees consistent feedback about progress. Employee satisfaction will improve if progress is well understood and feedback is consistent.

what later becomes a major investment in any of Nike's innovative customer-facing games like *Nike+* and *FuelBand* (both discussed in Chapter 8).

Ekins have long been the symbol of a deeply harmonious corporate culture. Nike has had a head start. And today, the alignment of the Nike brand with those who work for it is an enviable one. That's why, when you meet Ekins (evidenced by the swoosh on their leg) and you ask them what they do over at Nike, they will answer without flinching, "My job is to create a culture of joy around running."

Then they will smile like they actually mean it. Watch supporting videos and interact with your peers around ways to supercharge staff performance with *The Gamification Revolution* app, which you can download at http://gamrev.com.

Frontline Employees

This makes work feel like a game.

—Target Cashier

By the mid-2000s, Target customers had one major complaint: checkout lines. No matter how many additional registers the retail giant added to the front of its stores, it seemed there was nothing the company could do about the sluggishness of its cashiers. The old method—of adding and removing cashiers to match demand— could only do so much. Stores would still reach their breaking point during high seasons like Christmas, and turnover and training challenges were leading to staff and managerial burnout.

So Target did something surprising. The company added a game mechanic to the checkout experience. At the time, even those at Target's corporate offices weren't calling it a game. And most people wouldn't look at it from the outside and see it as "play." In fact, what has become known colloquially as the *Target Checkout Game* is simply the appearance of a letter on the screen as the cashier scans an item. The *Gs* and *Rs* (standing for green and red, respectively) indicate whether or not the space of time between each scan was fast enough—*G* for the right speed, *R* for too slow. At the end of the transaction, a percent appears on the screen (Figure 4.1). This number suggests an appropriate rate of speed per customer transaction, and it is in fact a total assessment of all the cumulative transactions that cashier has had in a given period.

FIGURE 4.1 Target used game mechanics to encourage staff to work more efficiently at the checkouts. The letter *G* (for green) increases the user's average, while the letter *R* (for red) decreases it.

Target gave the cashiers a suggested score of 82 percent, letting them know that scoring below that number could result in additional training, demotion, or even job loss. Scoring above, of course, would open advancement opportunities. But what happened next surprised everyone: not only did Target's checkout lines move faster than ever, but its cashiers reported an increase in satisfaction with their job experiences. The monotony and boredom often associated with the checkout experience suddenly had an injection of… fun. Employees themselves took personal pride in achieving a high score and, better still, beating it.

Target didn't build a virtual world. The company never offered prizes. In fact, the *Target Checkout Game* has by and large faded into the background and is now just a standard part of the checkout process, unremarkable by most accounts. Nevertheless, the game mechanics worked to give people doing a repetitive job a sense of control. It infused a level of competition similar to some casual games where the stakes are low and the challenges are simple. Through the act of play, there is a sense of accomplishment and therefore a desire to continue playing the game.

The behavioral concept behind this example is the idea of *agency*, which is the belief that you are in control of your own destiny. Agency is a simple and universal human need. Unsurprisingly, the World Health Organization (WHO) reports that one of the most significant stressors at work is a lack of control or choice over your work. This lack of control sets up a fundamental conflict for frontline employees, especially in the service sector. Generally, the work is monotonous, requires the employee to follow a defined set of procedures, and sets up inherent conflicts with the customers when their needs don't match the defined policies.

This conflict seems almost unresolvable, and it arises equally in any organization that interfaces with customers. This is why the Target example, and what the company *didn't* do, is more important than ever. Target *didn't* waste a ton of time and money making the cash register into a "Capital-G" Game. There were no dragons to slay, princesses to rescue, pigs to crush, or jewels to match.

GAMIFY YOUR READ

Choose Your Own Adventure— Solve Target's Checkout Problem Yourself!

By providing employees with a sense of agency, work feels less like work and more like a choice—which is fun. If you wanted to make your employees' experience more fun but still professional, choose your own adventure to solve Target's checkout problem!

Solution 1. Because the work of your checkout team has been sluggish and causing severe backups, you decide to motivate the staff by promising a pizza party after work one day in exchange for a little pep and faster service. (To see the results of this approach, turn to the answer key at the back of the book.)

Solution 2. You decide to punish your checkout team members for their poor performance by cutting five minutes off of their break time. You let all of them know that they are on probation and that if things don't pick up in line, they can expect to be replaced. (To see the results of this approach, turn to the answer key at the back of the book.)

Solution 3. You want to help your checkout staff members rally so you offer a weekly prize in the form of a $20 gift card for the individual who consistently gets the most customers through the checkout process in three minutes or less. Using the clock on the checkout computer, employees track their work by printing out a receipt at the end of each transaction. (To see the results of this approach, turn to the answer key at the back of the book.)

Instead of trying to make the work seem more exciting by making a game out of it, Target focused on giving the user instant feedback. And instead of directly tying compensation to the outcome, the company set a threshold and a target. Then they let the cashiers self-select the game. By doing so, they also continued to foster a sense of control, well summarized by this quote from a former Target cashier, Tessa, on an online forum: "It's a good system to keep the cashiers working and should be a message to everyone to not waste time while you're checking out."

This kind of support doesn't come naturally from the rank and file. By framing the feedback loop as being about individual performance and control, it made it possible to motivate people positively and to continuously drive up achievement without making the employees feel overly manipulated or like Big Brother was looking over their shoulders.

Motivating Managerial and Professional Staff

Cincinnati, Ohio–based Omnicare is one of the nation's leading pharmaceutical providers focused on the needs of long-term-care facilities like assisted living and nursing homes. The company operates a help desk service, providing round-the-clock assistance with software and hardware issues.

Because of the company's rapid growth, hold times and abandonment rates on the IT help desk support lines had reached unworkable numbers, with nearly 30 percent of all calls being dropped due to wait times of 20 minutes and longer. The company responded by implementing a new system that made call volumes, timing, and hold times into a more visible statistic by holding reps accountable for their performance. Rewards such as gift cards were offered to encourage good behavior as well. Unfortunately, rather than motivate a change for the better, a culture clash was born, and the incentives were met with major resistance.

The problem was simple: in the past if a caller asked the operator a question, providing the answer was a challenge in and of itself. While obviously more time-consuming, coming up with clever and effective tools, tips, and resources likely proved personally rewarding for the operators (and arguably more beneficial to the patient individuals who waited to get through to speak to them). However, if the operators were asked to go from creatively answering questions to answering those questions in a way designed to both speed things up and achieve prizes or points, motivation to comply would not necessarily outweigh the desire for personal satisfaction. And as this example shows, it proved more frustrating to the staff than beneficial.

The company responded, quickly realizing that the design of the system was improperly tuned to motivating the highly trained and already well-compensated employees manning the lines. They implemented the *OmniQuest* game based on *ServiceNow*—a cloud-based IT system designed to help manage the customer service process. *OmniQuest* was designed around a series of challenges and positive goals for the team members to meet, rather than nit-picky call-by-call modifiers. Core to the experience was a point system with badges for achieving key performance behaviors including good call-answer times and appropriate speed of query response.

Once redesigned, OmniCare saw immediate and significant improvement in both performance and morale. Staff members reacted positively, and both hold and dropoff rates declined by 80 percent over the redesign period. Anecdotal discussions with staff members also revealed that they really loved the challenges and quests that the system offered, even the games that were performance oriented, like "Get five perfect customer ratings in a row."

So why did raw scores and feedback work for the Target employees but fail miserably for the first iteration of the help desk? Why did the low-wage earners view the intervention as empowering, while the professional staff members found it demeaning and counterproductive? Moreover, the Target program carried no direct cash incentive, whereas the first version of the OmniCare program actually had gift cards and other tangible rewards associated with it. So why did the first version of the OmniCare program still underperform?

The answer is in how the employees fundamentally viewed their work. Where frontline cashiers felt highly regimented in their work and lacked feedback in the first place, IT help desk workers felt very empowered, and their roles were comparatively high status. After all, most help desk workers have to use their minds flexibly every day. So the introduction of specific goals, direct feedback, and simplistic rewards was automatically perceived as lowering agency rather than increasing it.

At the help desk, what was needed was a way to make the experience more engaging and unexpectedly rewarding. Effectively, instead of relying on external motivators (the customers' questions) to trigger activity, the company needed to make the reps' time more fun. By switching the focus of the gamified experience to individual performance challenges instead of focusing on the call-answer metrics alone, OmniCare still got to direct user behavior toward the positive outcomes it was seeking but without creating friction or frustration for the help desk operators.

From the ultimate success of the OmniCare example utilizing long-term goals and rewards, along with countless others, whole companies have emerged whose sole purpose is to generate successful employee engagement through gamification. Many of these companies are already delivering extraordinary results, transforming the employee experience and profoundly rethinking how the organizations themselves are actually structured.

Redesigning the Organization with Gamification

Toronto-based Rypple knows a thing or two about helping to reimagine organizational performance through gamification. The company, which was acquired by Salesforce.com in 2012 for an estimated $65 million and which is now called Work.com, pioneered the idea of making employee reviews into a mobile, social, and 360-degree function.

Realizing that the traditional, linear annual written review had lost its appeal in the current economic environment, the company re-engineered the process entirely. It built a suite of mobile and web apps that enabled the people inside an organization to provide instant feedback to their coworkers for a job well done. The system also allowed for decentralized goal setting, while maintaining top-line managerial control over the entire system. The results—which are displayed in a Facebook-style newsfeed and are supported by badges, leaderboards, and point systems—have enabled organizations to embrace social goal setting and performance development in ways that have been previously impossible. For the first time, users can send a note by writing publicly on a coworker's wall with messages as simple as, "Thanks for the help with that pitch. We won!"

Dynamic companies like Facebook, Gilt, Spotify, and Living-Social are among the bigger case studies of Salesforce.com's Work.com solution—and their results are astounding. LivingSocial is one such case in point. The daily-deals company delivers offers from half-price spa services to all-inclusive vacation packages to over 60 million members in 647 markets worldwide. Of their 4,900 employees, 98 percent have received at least one peer review using the system (often including some type of positive reinforcement like, "Nice job!"), and 93 percent have completed their own self-summaries. This statistic is even more astonishing when you factor in that the system was rolled out worldwide (adjusted for cultural differences) and was completely opt-in—in other words, no one was forced to join.

Giving, receiving, tracking, and reporting on feedback are the critical elements of performance enhancement systems within organizations. After all, if you want employees to do their best, they need to know what they are doing well (as well as what they are not doing well). Even more important, research shows that the sooner you give feedback after a "correctable" event, the better. Work.com and its competitors (like DueProps or PropsToYou) shorten the feedback loop to drive better results through continuous reinforcement from within the organization.

The benefits delivered by systems like Work.com and their competitors go well beyond just better feedback loops. The critical change they make is to turn the review process into something people actually *want* to do, thereby also increasing the amount and granularity of feedback. This "big data" stream allows managers to view the performance of people and teams and compare them in ways never before possible.

For example, through gamification, now employers can see much more than just when a salesperson closes a deal. Through the power of solutions like Work.com, they can actually follow the train to the other employees that helped get the deal closed. For example, the inside sales reps that took the first call, the tech support folks that answered key questions, the admins who scheduled appointments, the legal team that drew up the agreements, and so on. And each person can be easily viewed as an individual, a member of a team, or a part of a process—giving management a three-dimensional view of performance that was never before possible. Separately, these apps also help to reduce management overhead by making feedback into a crowdsourced activity.

Another way gamification helps scale performance is by reducing the cost of incentives. In most systems like PropsToYou, monetary compensation is, at most, a peripheral piece of the structure as a whole. The core concept is not to deliver gift cards or cash bonuses for every job well done but rather to use virtual rewards and point systems to track performance and roll that up—ultimately, into compensation—when it's appropriate and complete enough to make a difference. In the meantime, the introduction of instant feedback (for example, the Like button on Facebook) helps motivate people intrinsically to act out such positive behaviors as helping others and working hard. Whereas business once demonstrated its appreciation with cash and expensive prizes (like flashy vacations for top salespeople), now there is a widening range of rewards, and they come from your peers.

These socially driven rewards give management the ability to reinforce and motivate actions to which it would otherwise be difficult to assign a monetary value. For example, it's very challenging to adequately measure and reward "helpfulness" in a classic review system. With distributed, gamified reviews, we can score helpfulness based on what fellow employees consider important. By tracking these scores, recognition holds steady and quantifiable scores may continue to ascend.

Opting In

It bears repeating that the opt-in (as opposed to forced) nature of these systems, along with the ability to match a series of virtual rewards to the company's values, will ultimately lead to their adoption and use. In contrast, if gamified performance improvement is *required*, it will more than likely fall into the same trap as most other IT systems. In particular countries (and subgroups), it may also be viewed with suspicion. And while employees in frontline customer service are more amenable to strict feedback systems with clear key performance indicators (KPIs), knowledge workers, managers, and executives demand a more inclusive, user-centric, voluntary, and open-ended approach.

If you can tailor the solution to the problem, gamification will provide a unique opportunity to drive key performance metrics inside organizations of all sizes. Beyond driving performance, gamification can also increase employee satisfaction, recruitment efficacy, and—perhaps most important—innovation.

5

IGNITING EMPLOYEE INNOVATION

★

When you think of employee-driven innovation, federal governments are rarely the first thing that comes to mind. But in the United Kingdom, the Department for Work and Pensions (DWP) has become one of the leaders in driving innovative ideas from within its own ranks. The agency's gamified economic marketplace for innovation, called *Idea Street,* has been spreading employee ideas and then turning them into realities—and the timing couldn't be any better (Figure 5.1). In the midst of the austerity programs gripping Europe, the DWP is still the United Kingdom's largest government agency. The agency accounts for nearly 28 percent of the nation's budget, spending £121 billion (over $190 billion) and delivering a range of services—including the design and implementation of welfare and pension policies and programs—through 120,000 civil servants.

The premise of *Idea Street* is relatively simple: users propose innovations that they would like to see the DWP implement. These range from straightforward ideas such as "add e-mail signatures to every outgoing e-mail" to community improvement plans like "develop a train-the-trainer program" and others ranging across the spectrum of activities in which the DWP is engaged. The best ideas are then curated and turned into assets that can be traded, as on a stock market. Employees buy or sell shares in the best ideas,

FIGURE 5.1 The U.K. Department for Work and Pensions (DWP) created *Idea Street* as a way to allow staff members to propose innovative ideas and vote for the best ones.

driving the prices up and down as a proxy for their quality— as well as contributing additional ideas to each as it progresses. Top concepts are then vetted by the organization itself and, when appropriate, implemented. The entire system is backed by a virtual currency.

In the first 9 months of play, *Idea Street* delivered a measurable savings of over £10 million (approximately $16 million). This represented the net value to the department of 60 different ideas running over an 18-month time horizon. In any governmental department, this pace of innovation and cost savings without service cuts is unprecedented. But as the program's successes continue to mount, it's the human response that has been even more exciting. Civil servants report increased job satisfaction because they feel listened to, and customers report greater happiness due to improved service quality. By using a gamified marketplace design, the organization has cut the red tape and facilitated the movement of ideas—and as a result, "capital"—to focus on quality. Novel, indeed.

And the genius of the game isn't even the visible end result but rather the classic motivator that is missing: specifically, cash. Despite the robust market activity taking place every day, DWP employees cannot turn their winnings into cash of any kind. The virtual economy in *Idea Street* stays virtual—the principal rewards from playing the game are bragging rights on a leaderboard and having a sense of contribution.

That noncash design didn't come naturally to the creator of *Idea Street*, Dr. James Gardner. Dr. Gardner was the chief technologist for the DWP, an expert on innovation and a banker whose background emphasized the importance of cash to motivate behavior. Instead, it was the lesson he learned as head of innovation for Lloyds TSB, the (pre-2008 financial crisis) British banking giant, that illuminated it for him.

There, Gardner pioneered a game called *Innovation Market,* the precursor to *Idea Street.* Called upon by the CEO to unlock innovation potential in the bank's hundreds of thousands of frontline

The Problem with Cash

Cash rewards often negatively distort user behavior, and ultimately they make the game more difficult. Over time, players will simply consider it their rightful due (consider how everyone feels about a paycheck). Thus the cash reward must be constantly increased in order to drive the same behavior. Over time, costs to maintain the game will be driven up while user satisfaction plummets. Cash isn't the strong motivator over the long term that you might expect. Behavior experts from Abraham Maslow (the famed psychologist) to Daniel Pink (author of *Drive*) have repeatedly emphasized the need for noncash rewards in order to maintain momentum and engagement. Delivering noncash prizes such as status, access, and power will extend the life of your game, save you money, and drive better results.

employees, he architected the game in much the same way—a virtual marketplace for ideas—with startlingly different results. Instead of focusing on noncash rewards, the *Innovation Market*'s activity was based on a virtual currency called "banker beans," which were backed by real money.

The idea generation and implementation he achieved was—and probably still is—unparalleled. At its peak, *Innovation Market* was generating over 1,200 ideas per month, many of which were implemented quickly by the bank. In its biggest win, the market surfaced a small flaw in Lloyd's loan application system that had been costing the bank millions of pounds per month. After uncovering and fixing just that single flaw, *Innovation Market's* internal rate of return (IRR) moved permanently into positive territory.

But the real-world rewards had a downside. The introduction of real currency led to speculation, market manipulation, and hyperinflation. Gardner tried to tamp down the behavior by introducing such classic measures as price controls and taxation—both of which resulted in extreme player dissatisfaction. While *Innovation Market* was, in spite of its flawed reward system, fun to play, the complications and ultimate ballooning expense of the game made its viability questionable for the long run. Meanwhile, when building *Idea Street*, Gardner focused on building a meaningful player experience, but he did so by creating an environment in which the meaning was in the game itself and not the external reward. Both games were fun, offering a unique opportunity for players to experience public success inside their organization. But *Idea Street*, with its use of virtual (noncash) rewards, was sustainable and continues to be played to this day—delivering millions in savings at almost no expense to the DWP.

The lesson is clear, economic simulation games—like *Innovation Market* and *Idea Street*—can be powerful tools, delivering innovation from the people with the best view of how to improve your company: your employees. Organizations that use gamification to motivate employee innovation can inspire a true and meaningful alignment between your brand and those who work for it. By staying away from cash incentives, you create a powerful long-term program at little cost.

Today, Dr. Gardner continues his mission as an innovation guru through invaluable books, such as *Sidestep & Twist*, and as a senior executive for Spigit. As he will quickly tell you, there is no Cupid's arrow for driving innovation in organizations, but gamification presents a unique, dynamic, and scalable opportunity to engage employees in the process. Gamification has been so successful at driving employee innovation that Gartner Group's Elise Olding forecasts that by 2015, 25 percent of all business process management (BPM) systems will use gamification in some way. And Gartner's Brian Burke says 70 percent of the Global 2,000—the largest corporations—will use it to drive innovation.

In surveying the landscape of the leaders in this field, you will quickly find there is an order to gamification implementation. Gamification leverages three key strategic approaches to drive corporate innovation:

- ➤ Marketplaces and competition
- ➤ Simulations
- ➤ Play

By examining each more closely, we can begin to build a picture of how you too can use gamification to drive innovation.

Marketplaces and Competition

Both *Idea Street* and *Innovation Market*, profiled above, make use of the marketplace design for gamified innovation. One of the main keys to the designs' overall successes was an accelerated feedback loop. A *feedback loop* is a system by which users' output yields feedback that in turn loops them back in to uncover the nature of the feedback. On completion of a feedback loop, users can then incorporate this input into their next decision, making it easier to move forward. Social networking has made feedback loops something of an everyday occurrence for anyone interacting with them. In

GAMIFY YOUR READ

Mad Libs

Read the words beneath the blanks to a coworker or friend (or ask someone to read them to you!), and then fill in the blanks with the answers provided. Read the *Mad Lib* with the individual's words filled in for a hilarious take on fostering employee motivation and creativity.

Many say that _____ storming is the best way to come
              [BODY ORGAN]

up with _____ new ideas for your company. However,
     [ADJECTIVE]

_____ is implementing some _____ _____ meth-
[A BUSINESS]   [ADJECTIVE]   [ADJECTIVE]

ods that promise to _____ their business so that it is the
                [VERB]

_____.
[SUPERLATIVE–MOST LIKELY TO . . .]

   It all started when _____ saw
                     [NAME OF SOMEONE YOU HAVE WORKED FOR]

how _____ conducted business. That man-
     [A COWORKER YOU HAVE ADMIRED]

ager knew that beating _____ was more important than
            [A TECH COMPANY]

getting the highest _____ in a game.
           [NOUN]

   By talking to as many _____ as possible, the _____
                [PLURAL NOUN]   [JOB TITLE]

weighed every _____ before deciding on _____ as the
       [NOUN]   [BUSINESS TREND]

best way to improve _____ and obtain the best _____ strat-
         [NOUN]   [ADJECTIVE]

egies. Additionally, in order to make people's _____, the
                          [PLURAL NOUN]

business asked its _____ to _____ and _____ as often as
        [PLURAL NOUN] [VERB]   [VERB]

possible to improve their _____ . The business organized a _____
                          [NOUN]   [SPORT]

team and asked people to _____ .
                          [VERB]

Soon, everyone was _____ , and no one wanted to go back
                    [EMOTION]

to _____ when everyone was wearing _____
   [YEAR]   [AN OLD-FASHIONED ARTICLE

_____ and _____ . Today everyone at _____
OF CLOTHING]   [BRAND OF SHOE]   [NAME OF A BUSI-

_____ is _____ and _____ , and the business is _____ .
NESS]   [ADJECTIVE]   [ADJECTIVE]   [ADJECTIVE]

Visit the companion app for *The Gamification Revolution* at
http://gamrev.com and unlock bonus content, interact with your
peers, and leverage resources to make gamified innovation a
core part of your business.

the case of a feedback loop on Twitter, users tweet status updates. Followers of the user respond to the updates, which then brings the user back to Twitter in order to read and respond to those responses. Similarly, the design of the feedback loop in *Idea Street* allows for praise and critical commentary around any given idea. An idea's "stock price" (based on popular interest) gives value to each and becomes the source of the feedback.

In old-fashioned feedback models, new ideas might have to wait weeks for a hastily drawn performance review. However, modern feedback loops allow for commentary that is not only immediate but also transparent and *relevant*. This approach also encourages collaboration and constructive competition, rather than cutthroat economics or passive-aggressive behavior.

Avoiding blame and negative competition served as the primary challenge for Microsoft's quality assurance (QA) teams. For a service that error-checked millions of lines of code per year, the teams were responsible for the reputation of billions of dollars' worth of applications. The QA function is typically viewed by developers as a chore. Unsurprisingly, like any author, they prefer the process of the creation over the editing. The inherent struggles were endless in motivating them to complete necessary but tedious tasks like bug discovery or fixing existing code.

With the arrival of Windows 7, everything changed. Suddenly billions of dollars hinged on the success of these millions of lines of code. Given the waning interest in its products, Microsoft knew it had to get it right. Even worse, the software would release globally. Although code itself is universal, a global release must account for the language discrepancies from English to Swahili when it comes to what the user sees. Known as *localization*, this process needs to be highly accurate and clear to ensure a smooth upgrade. Typically, this painstaking work is farmed out to language localization companies where high costs and latency impact both budgets and time.

Seeking a new, faster, and more cost-effective way to resolve this issue, Microsoft turned to Ross Smith—an internal champion of gamification for a solution. Smith proposed the *Windows Language Quality Game*—and changed the face of software localization forever (Figure 5.2).

The basic premise was this: within Microsoft's employee base of over 90,000 people, it was safe to assume there would be native-level language speakers of almost every dialect—or at least most of the ones they needed. Perhaps those individuals could help test and refine the interface? But attempting to force, cajole, or beg disparate employees—who might be in the mailroom, lunchroom, or boardroom—to voluntarily spend time reviewing interfaces seemed pretty likely to fail. So Ross turned to gamification, and the results were astonishing.

Over the course of the game, 4,600 players contributed feedback on over half a million screens within the app—finding nearly 7,000 defects. The game was designed to leverage players' free time by giving them small challenges they could complete in a few minutes

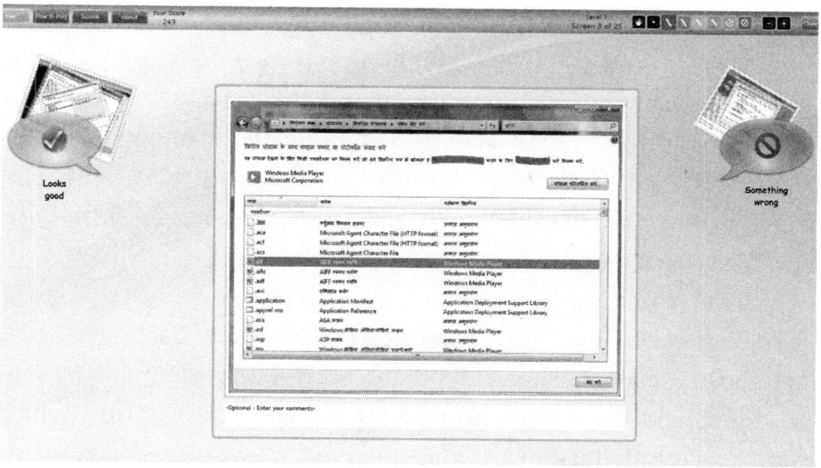

FIGURE 5.2 *Windows Language Quality Game* was Microsoft's innovation game used to motivate staff to help find glitches before the launch of Windows 7.

a day. Running the game would present players with a screenshot of Windows 7 in their language of choice. Players could then circle items that needed review, submit proposed localizations, and vote on proposals submitted by other players. Points were awarded for effort and peer-reviewed accuracy. Language teams were also ranked on a leaderboard.

Beyond just the cash and time saved, the approach allowed the company to raise the overall quality of its software. The company could also build a rapport with smaller language-speaking populations that might have otherwise seen significant errors in a first release. But the best part was that employees rallied around a new, large-scale task that everyone agreed was exciting to complete. This excitement and engagement is critical to the success of knowledge-intensive tasks. Although research shows that all kinds of workers respond well to enthusiasm and agency, nowhere is this more important than with high-value employees.

Ross, who runs a program through Microsoft called 42Projects, which works to raise productivity through gamification, understood this dynamic all too well. He anticipated that employees would respond particularly well to the "tribal challenge" design of the experience, whereby each language-speaking population came together as a team. Along with seeing their performances on a global leaderboard, Ross also believed that the teams would view the opportunity to perfect the software for their own "tribes" as an "epic win" that would benefit their home countries—something meaningful to motivate involvement and pride.

The way the game propelled users through the interface, or the "progress mechanics" of the game, was also key. Each challenge, principally asking users to look at a screen and identify any language errors, was broken up into segments of 25 at a time, which were represented as levels. Players could also earn achievements including new pen colors for annotating text within the body of the game to signify a higher skill set as they progressed.

Even more critically, and especially within the culture of a large organization, the main form of positive feedback was that the company was listening. Periodically, users would receive reports that showed how the bugs they found were being fixed. This sense that their contribution was ultimately worthwhile and having a positive effect on the organization was a key motivating factor in success.

Closing the Feedback Gap

When you compare the near-immediate feedback of the *Windows Language Quality Game* with the disconnected and frequently complex formulas used for "companywide bonus calculations," you can easily see what's missing from the old-fashioned model. Most of the old calculations tried to divide performance by contribution and tenure. They rarely considered an individual's unique performance. Given that alone, it's easy to see why a shorter-loop feedback system is so popular among the rank and file.

Closing the feedback gap and bringing it closer to frontline teams was a pressing objective at Citibank when it hired Susan Andrews from Apple in 2010. Brought on to lead innovation at the company, Andrews's bosses hoped her Apple experience would

Design Competitions: Gamification at Work

Can you imagine allocating between $50,000 and $80,000 in staff commitments and resources in order to conceive a revolutionary design at which you have—maybe—one in several hundred chances of winning? What if, in addition to intricate renderings of your design, you must also strategize a project from top to bottom including its budget and scope? And *then,* what if elements of your proposed design could become the intellectual property of the client, whether or not you win, whose only obligation is to mention that you "inspired" the final product? Would you enter?

Although it might seem counterintuitive, some of the world's most famous landmarks and public spaces have one thing in common: they were first conceived in a game. The London Olympic Legacy Park, New York City's Governor's Island, the Barcelona Museum of Contemporary Art, and the High Line all prove that design competitions are thriving. Enthusiastic participation along with the investment of copious resources is par for the course.

What is remarkable about design competitions is how they are so widely embraced by the architecture industry as a whole. In fact, some competitions are intentionally anonymous in order to level the playing field and allow new talent to float to the top. And the promise of prestige is sometimes all the motivation participants need to get involved.

For clients of design, the benefits of competition are obvious and include the proffering of many ideas for one project. For new designers it presents a chance to level up and achieve visibility. For those already established in their discipline, past wins bring about invitations to more prestigious and more lucrative private competitions. For the world at large they make it possible to bear witness to the future of design. From a gamification standpoint it would seem there are no losers.

help inject momentum and innovation into their slow-moving, ailing institution with its $1.4 trillion in assets and heightened government oversight. Her first priority was to establish a 25-person innovation team in Palo Alto, California. The team's first project was called the *Global Ideas Challenge.* The game would leverage the creative power of Citi's hundreds of thousands of employees, and the hope was that it would lead to meaningful change.

Out of the gate more than 20 percent of those approached to participate got involved. The way the company broke down collaboration was that 10 percent offered ideas to the system and were named "ideators." Upwards of 50 percent became "collaborators" who added to or amended those ideas. Finally, a group of people called "connectors" got others involved in the program by reaching out to individuals they assessed would be helpful or would enjoy the process. Ultimately, more than 2,300 ideas were generated from 97 countries. Although Citi has remained tight-lipped about what those ideas were, four ideas were presented to Citi's top management, and one was selected to be executed by the company.

Andrews learned from her time at Apple how to engage not only her consumer base but her employee base as well. Apple's well-respected innovation techniques include top-down, bottom-up strategizing and the fundamental principle that creativity begins by asking questions. In fact, the company believes that more questions net better answers. According to EBTIC's case study of Apple's innovative strategies, "Innovation is what happens when you find answers." Apple's pesky tendency to disrupt the market time and again and thereby change it time and again proves that they are leading innovation, not by guessing, but by *engaging.*

When Andrews arrived at Citibank, the company had fallen from industry leader (Citibank was the first to offer ATMs and online banking) to just trying to keep its head above water in the wake of the banking crisis. Now it is becoming an innovator once again by redesigning not just the banking experience but the bank itself. Reimagined in what some are comparing to the style of an

Apple store, Citibanks of the future will be almost entirely auto-mated. A new app was launched in 2011 designed to help propel Citibank closer to creating a revolutionary banking experience for their users—one in which customers become their own bankers by learning the industry from the inside out. By simulating a real-world banking experience, users get to "play" banker in order to learn the best ways to save and grow their bank accounts.

Of course, few would argue that Citibank—or the banking indus-try at large—can claim to be innovators in employee engagement. But the global economic crisis, coupled with increasing internal and external pressure, is helping to remake the banking industry. Often it's not the most gamelike businesses that have the most success with gamification but rather those that *need* it the most.

Innovating the Future

This demand for innovation in a large, slow-moving, and regulated environment also drove the overarching design of the Race to the Top (R2T) program—a $4.35 billion contest developed under Presi-dent Obama in 2009 and run by the Department of Education to spur innovation in state-level educational policy.

The basic concept of R2T is that states can earn points for enact-ing particular educational reforms designed to enhance teacher and school accountability, technical infrastructure, and standards of curriculum. The program grades regions and states on a curve, publishing their scores so they can compare performance. The bet-ter each state does relative to the others at each round, the more of the money they get.

The competitive and financial incentives are helping to drive massive reform, with some states like Hawaii moving from low scores to the top of the heap on measures of preparedness and modernity in only a year. School districts across the country have held rallies to support the program, bringing parents, students, and teachers together to raise awareness and team spirit to fix up and modernize schools. The competitive, market-oriented reforms, by and large, are having their desired effect. For example, California now allows student performance data to be linked to teacher and school performance data, enabling leaderboards and comparisons at every level. And Austin, Texas, has developed a point-based compensation system that rewards teachers based on student outcomes and other activities, such as peer mentoring.

What we don't know about R2T, of course, is whether or not it improves actual student outcomes. The program hasn't run for long enough, and its outcomes data has yet to be made available. It does highlight, however, how gamification can be used to achieve an objective that's a proxy for the underlying goal—in this case school preparedness for student achievement. The key is to define the metrics for the goals of the business and also for their trackability and achievability. Successive federal government administrations have tried to modernize schools by persuasion. From bottomless funds for computers to anti-asbestos laws, they've done just about everything. But challenging the whole school community—its parents, teachers, administrators, and students—was what the system needed to work.

Just like R2T, change needs to start somewhere. Making it easier to analyze the performance of our projects and eliciting a clear understanding of their tangible goals (including actual numbers), along with having a means to collect and analyze data about them, are critical underpinnings to producing breakthroughs with gamification.

Simulations

Sometimes marketplaces can't adequately drive innovation in a gamified context. This may be because the scenarios are either too complex or specific to engage large crowds or because users may not be able to truly see the opportunities until they are playing with systems directly.

Those situations demand a simulation-oriented design. The number of employee simulation games for innovation has been wildly proliferating. Nowhere more so than at NTT Data—Japan's largest IT services company and one of the world's largest business process outsourcing consultancies.

The company's head of internal innovation, Naureen Meraj, helped develop a simulation called *Go Leadership*—that helps the company's disparate team members drive client innovation. A large percentage of the company's 58,000 consultants work on site with clients, often spending 5, 10, or even 25 years as separate but equal parts of client teams. The devotion and stability of the company's workforce are part of why NTT Data has been able to generate over $14 billion per year in revenues, despite being a standalone entity only since 1988.

However, this kind of familiarity comes at a price. Consultants who spend too long at customer sites are said to have "gone native," identifying more with the client than with NTT Data—their actual employer. Such deep alignment between consultant and customer might at first seem ideal. But as innovation becomes ever more important, an overly familiar consultant can quickly turn to dead-weight. After all, the company often hires these outsiders in the first place precisely to ensure fresh thinking and innovation.

For their part, long-term consultants often report feeling "stuck" in their jobs. Isolated somewhere between one employer and another, these once-motivated and thriving individuals enter their own Twilight Zone. Feeling part of neither culture, divorced from their path to progress and innovation, these employees rarely achieve the innovation and efficiency objectives that NTT Data and the client expect.

So here lies the natural tension: How do you get consultants deeply embedded in their host organization to avoid losing their edge?

You give them *Go*—NTT's Gamified Innovation Solution.

The project to gamify began years earlier when Meraj, originally trained as a guidance counselor, started gamifying interactions at NTT. She began with simple icebreaking games and innovation catalysts at meetings—such as those described in Chapter 3's section on Gamestorming. Soon, she added little games meant to drive enhanced creativity and foster cross-cultural communication. As the organization slowly awoke to the power of gamification, the Seattle native found herself spearheading a major initiative. Given only a little over 12 months from original concept to execution, Meraj's *Go Leadership* game uses a virtual world to help consultants rise up in the ranks *in the real world.*

By giving them tests, quizzes, and challenges that begin on the topic of shared values, and eventually progressing to virtual-world interactions, these simulations challenge consultants to deal with emergency scenarios, like difficult employees and client relationship issues. *Go* is designed to both coach employees on how to do better in complex situations as they progress to management (or along other career tracks) and to test their mettle. The better you perform in *Go*, the more opportunities you'll receive for advancement and bonuses in your real job. By carefully engaging NTT's upper management, Meraj has been able to connect virtual- and real-world outcomes, raising the stakes—and excitement all around.

The company has also turned gamification into a center of excellence (COE)—leveraging the work done with *Go Leadership* into the *Go Platform.* Like many of the COE examples in Chapter 2, NTT Data now wants to export its internal gamification to serve their clients. Unlike other internal gamification programs being turned outward, *Go* has been designed to allow for game modules to be created on the fly to address unique client needs. For example, if consultants are struggling with a banking client's accounts payable process, *Go* can be used to quickly create a training and performance game that addresses that specific issue.

In the game, consultants might be faced with a total computer meltdown, a vendor insisting on payment for invoices already paid, or major cash flow pressure from upper management. In every case, the right answers and processes can be based on the specific client's real-life approach, so that the challenge is unique and applicable. By making it easy to bring real-world scenarios into the game, NTT Data hopes to gain a significant advantage over competitors in terms of quality and consultant flexibility.

A wide range of companies use gamified simulation to drive innovation results, including major brands such as Nike, which has developed a supply-chain simulation game to drive meaningful eco-understanding throughout the company. Governments like the city of San Jose and the state of North Carolina are using them to come up with innovative plans for balancing budgets. Entire companies like ExperiencePoint and IDEO offer organizations tailored workshops that are specifically about innovation through simulation.

Meanwhile, more visceral and emotional gamified techniques are simultaneously taking hold. Principal among these is—play. Yes, *that* play. The one you remember from recess or summer nights. It's a simple concept but one whose place in work and innovation continues to be both controversial and particularly effective.

Play

Play is broadly defined as any activity we engage in for the purposes of recreation or enjoyment. The very word itself seems like it would be so out of place in the work environment. However, mounting evidence proves that it is both restorative and highly useful for driving innovation and excellence *in the work environment.* Yet somehow play still gets a bad rap for being trivial or... well... the opposite of "work."

Research and analysis have shown many benefits from using play to drive innovation. In his landmark work on play through the lens of drug discovery, researcher Alexander Styhre has highlighted how the elements of chance and skill in games and play help drive creativity and innovation. Academic analyses—such as David Abramis's *Play in Work* (1990)—have reinforced our understanding that certain kinds of play (notably, games) enhance our sense of work success, while other kinds feel unrelated to progress at the office.

The fundamental tension between work, innovation, and play extends beyond just definitions. The problem with play is that when it is forced or goal specific, it tends not to serve its purpose—relaxation, creativity, connectedness, recharging. So how do leading organizations resolve this conflict to get good results from play? By designing game systems around Abramis's observation that *play from games* generally produces the best work-related results. Therefore, when we need unstructured play to regenerate our creative juices, we can use it in short bursts to fuel our innovation batteries.

San Francisco–based Woopaah is a start-up focused on just that challenge. Founded by Stella Grizont, Woopaah uses the elements of positive psychology and imagination to create a "playground" for executives to learn, connect, and recharge. The experience—which involves a range of activities from traversing a sheer mazelike room as a team to creating art with strangers—is designed to deliver the positive reinforcement and creative "stretching" that stressed and busy individuals so often lack.

This is precisely what Google meant when it pioneered its 70/20/10 model of innovation. Former CEO Eric Schmidt suggested that 70 percent of employee time should be spent on core business tasks, 20 percent on core business projects (also known as *innovation time off*), and 10 percent on things unrelated to the business. The discretionary time—a well-known "perk" of Google's highly engineer-focused culture—is responsible for some of Google's most successful new products. Ideas generated during the playful innovation time off include GMail, Google News, Google Talk, and AdSense. By creating time for employees to play with ideas in a "safe" space (for example, no punishment from management

See how Woopaah works, what mistakes *Idea Street* designer James Gardner made, and dozens more innovation experts discussing what it takes to spark genius. Go online to expand and share your thoughts about innovation with *The Gamification Revolution* app, which can be downloaded at http://gamrev.com.

for experimenting), Google helps foster a culture that has been extraordinarily innovative.

Google's campus is filled with games employees can play, including beach volleyball and pool—and Google is not the only one touting "recess" as the new "smoke break." Although often the butt of jokes, the homely foosball table and Xbox 360 in the breakroom of Silicon Valley lore are now standard issue in most dynamic organizations.

Riley Gipson, CEO of social start-up Napkin Labs, is a believer in the power of play to drive innovation. Writing on this subject in *Inc.* magazine, he said, "Kids are super creative. Why? Because when they play, there is no limit to their imaginations. At Napkin Labs, when we have a problem to solve, we often try to step back and emulate a child-like state of mind, essentially ignoring reality. Yes, many of the ideas put forward will never work, but the act of stretching our minds often times leads to a breakthrough."

Like Napkin Labs, IDEO is another company that has had major success with the concept of applying "structured" play to innovation. Founded through a merger of design firms in 1991, IDEO is known the world over as one of the leading industrial, product, and experience design companies. A consistent winner of design competitions like the prestigious *Bloomberg Businessweek* and Industrial Designers Society of America (IDSA) annual Industrial Design Excellence Awards (IDEA), IDEO consults to a wide swath of the world's biggest and most innovative organizations. Not surprisingly then, IDEO's chief executive Tim Brown believes in play.

The company often uses role-playing as a research method for design. Famously, during a project to redesign healthcare experiences, IDEO designers checked themselves into hospitals as sick patients. What they quickly discovered was that hours of patient time were spent—from triage to discharge—staring at the ceiling, listening to muffled voices. The video of the experience has been used to teach user-centered design for a wide range of applications. More specifically, it has become a rallying cry to redesign hospital workflow in a patient-centered way.

IDEO also uses playful competition—like a holiday gingerbread decorating contest—to stimulate lateral thinking and encourage new kinds of employee interactions. Similarly, the company believes in giving employees some random time off, to go see a sporting event together, for example. By creating a space for play that creates surprise and delight, IDEO gets the best of both worlds: a way to foster innovation and team building that is cheap, easy, and fun.

Though the kinds of play that are acceptable will vary from company to company, the core message is clear: play helps people excel. Far from being a throwaway perk, it balances the stress of the modern work world and creates open spaces to drive innovation. How will your organization make space for play? It doesn't cost much to try—and the potential is virtually unlimited.

Gamification is rapidly becoming a key element in innovation's strategic arsenal. By using designs as varied as marketplaces, simulations, and pure play, companies of all sizes are crafting work environments that deliver ideas—and results. Clearly, it also helps to build corporate climates that many employees consider appealing, which lends gamification another critical win—as a driver of recruitment and retention.

6

REIMAGINING RECRUITMENT, TRAINING, AND DEVELOPMENT

★

n 1983, the United States began what would become a profound period of economic growth. This in turn spurred business development across sectors, increased educational opportunities for American youth, and created an ultimate surplus in tax revenue for our government. In fact, from the looks of things, everyone in the 1980s was happy, prosperous, and using far too much hairspray— from the Ewings on TV's *Dallas* to the Joneses next door.

But one entity was suffering: the American military. Due to an expansive breadth of opportunities for the 18- to 25-year-old male, no one wanted to volunteer for a service that relied exclusively on people *wanting to volunteer*. With no real conflict other than a simmering Cold War being fought mostly at an ideological level, recruiting people under the guise of "duty" was no longer resonating with American youth.

The Army, in an attempt to rebrand itself as an "adventure" as opposed to a "responsibility," launched a campaign encouraging you to "Be all that you can be." Still, recruitment remained sluggish into the 1990s, at which point it had become practically mercenary in nature, promising scholarships and otherwise bank-rolling expensive recruitment practices.

As mentioned in Chapter 2, when *America's Army* was launched in 2002 by retired colonel Casey Wardynski, Army recruitment became forever changed. Using computer game technology, *America's Army* provided players with a virtual Army experience. The game was explicitly designed not to convert players to recruits immediately but rather—in Colonel Wardynski's words—to "put the U.S. Army into the discussion when high school grads were thinking about careers."

But there was an exciting additional boon: engaging the recruits in this manner eventually led to lower acquisition costs, and *America's Army* became the most cost-effective recruitment project in the military's history. Over the course of 10 years, the game cost a total of $33 million to build, and maintenance costs were substantially lower—ultimately a small drop in the $700 million annual recruitment budget of the armed forces. Over that period, the Army claimed in sworn congressional testimony that *America's Army* was more effective than any other approach at connecting with recruits. In 2008, the Massachusetts Institute of Technology (MIT) researched the results of the game, and it found that 30 percent of young Americans had a more favorable opinion of the Army directly because of the game and that it had a greater impact on recruits than all other forms of Army advertising *combined*. With more than 9 million downloads, *America's Army* remained listed in the top 10 for first-person shooter games for years.

What's more, players expressed an understanding of what it meant to be in the Army. And the new recruits who had played the game were far more likely to make it through the first nine volatile weeks of basic training. The game had prepared them in a way that no commercial, no slogan, no poster of a pointing Uncle Sam had ever been able to do.

Meanwhile, these new recruits benefited the Army itself by arriving with some idea about where they belonged in the system, and in some cases, with preliminary training. For example, to become an

Army medic in the game world, players had to go through specialized training. While the training was specific to a virtual reality, one player, Paxton Galvanek, saved lives when he successfully triaged the scene of a car accident after he had served as a medic in the game. He had no previous medical training or experience.

But *America's Army* is a complex game that required years of development and thousands of production hours. Not all great gamified recruitment ideas need to be so expansive. What made *America's Army* such an unmitigated success was its draw: fun. Players liked the game, and any ancillary benefit to the Army itself, at least from the players' standpoint, was incidental at best. By making a game—or a challenge—fun, attracting players becomes substantially easier.

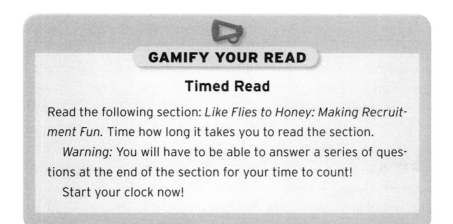

GAMIFY YOUR READ

Timed Read

Read the following section: *Like Flies to Honey: Making Recruitment Fun*. Time how long it takes you to read the section.

Warning: You will have to be able to answer a series of questions at the end of the section for your time to count!

Start your clock now!

Like Flies to Honey: Making Recruitment Fun

In 2004, Google placed a billboard in Silicon Valley that stated "{first 10-digit prime found in consecutive digits e}.com." There was no mention of Google at all on the billboard—and while most non-math geeks likely drove on by with little more than a raised eyebrow, the mathematically curious (who actually mattered to Google) had their interests piqued. The answer to the puzzle, "7427466391.com," led users to another blank page containing another mathematical puzzle to solve. If users were successful once more, then they were taken to a Google Labs page where they read the following: "One thing we learned while building Google is that it's easier to find what you're looking for if it comes looking for you. What we're looking for are the best engineers in the world. And here you are."

The reward for their efforts: a pretty powerful compliment from the world's leading software company. Not too shabby! This "secret" recruiting tool delivered in the form of a puzzle ensured that those who attempted to solve it actually had a personal and vested interest in the challenge. The average person would not bother to solve—much less figure out—a random mathematical equation placed on a billboard, which is exactly what Google wanted: an atypical math enthusiast and problem solver!

By attracting the right applicants through its billboard challenge, Google was able to kick off its recruitment efforts with a solid base of uncommonly qualified candidates. Gamification is so effective as a recruitment tool principally because it is capable of helping organizations filter candidates in (and out) at an extraordinary scale, and moreover, because gamified recruitment allows the best companies to demonstrate to top candidates that they are fun and engaging places to work from the get-go—a critical strategy in competitive markets. Google's model was so successful at delivering quality engineers that the challenge has been repeatedly emulated and re-imagined by other companies hoping to achieve the same results.

For example, Quixey, a search engine for smartphone apps, was similarly looking for employees from engineering and tech backgrounds. Like Google, the company decided against hiring costly recruiters to solve its problem and instead created the *Quixey Challenge.* However, rather than relying on the mere curiosity of passersby, Quixey set up the game on a website and explicitly offered a cash prize of $100 to draw visitors. Players had to solve three practice problems before being able to try the real challenge—solving an algorithm bug in under one minute in front of a Skype audience. In December 2011, the challenge had 38 winners. From that pool, 5 serious candidates were considered for open positions. The entire

Risk and Reward

Obviously, Quixey took a risk with its design. But in a well-designed gamified system, you should have control over the execution of the program. For example, you need the ability to cap the number of players, limit their attempts, or even adjust the incoming requests through an invitation-only approach. With high rates of fraud and cheating, it's impossible to predict everything people will do up front. The best way of dealing with any potential risk is to have a great *Terms of Service* (TOS) and smart people managing the process. In this way, gamification can actually increase your explicit control over a challenging situation (like recruitment) by highlighting bad behavior early and often.

Quixey isn't the only company that has used gamification in an edgy way—and won. Access the companion app to *The Gamification Revolution* at http://gamrev.com. You will find exclusive video of leading designers sharing their passions and pitfalls—and learn how not to make the same mistake twice.

enterprise cost Quixey a mere $3,800 to find top-notch recruits, where by comparison, standard recruiting fees would have easily exceeded $100,000 using traditional methods.

Beyond just the cost savings, Quixey also gained an important cultural tool: by making the contest public, winners gained a shared sense of identity through the exercise, increasing their alignment with the company and each other. Such team building exercises—even before people have officially become a *team*—can deliver substantial benefits over time, especially in a start-up setting with intense work demands. Even more, finding an effective way to sift through the mountains of potential recruits within a manageable and deliberate setting could land your company on a path miles ahead of the competition. And by utilizing the power of gamification, you might realize you can find the best talent where you least expect it...

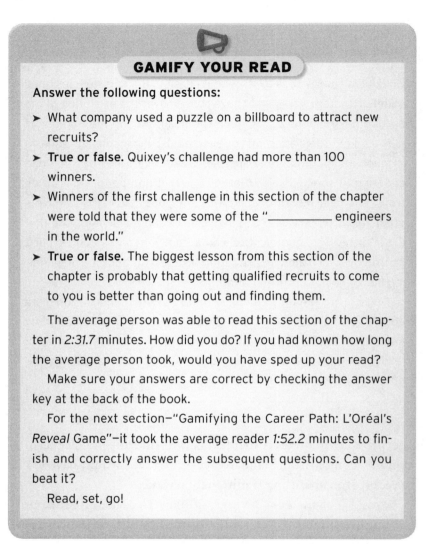

Answer the following questions:

➤ What company used a puzzle on a billboard to attract new recruits?

➤ **True or false.** Quixey's challenge had more than 100 winners.

➤ Winners of the first challenge in this section of the chapter were told that they were some of the "_____ engineers in the world."

➤ **True or false.** The biggest lesson from this section of the chapter is probably that getting qualified recruits to come to you is better than going out and finding them.

The average person was able to read this section of the chapter in *2:31.7* minutes. How did you do? If you had known how long the average person took, would you have sped up your read?

Make sure your answers are correct by checking the answer key at the back of the book.

For the next section—"Gamifying the Career Path: L'Oréal's *Reveal* Game"—it took the average reader *1:52.2* minutes to finish and correctly answer the subsequent questions. Can you beat it?

Read, set, go!

Gamifying the Career Path: L'Oréal's *Reveal* Game

More graduates than ever are leaving universities still uncertain about where they might fit in after college. Younger potential job candidates are interested in flexibility and choice in terms of when and how they work. There is less interest in traditional working environments, sitting at a desk, working their way up the corporate ladder. Younger recruits expect to achieve as much meaning in their working life as they have in their lives outside the office. And for them, a game that can help them achieve a meaningful career path is a valuable asset for the businesses hoping to hire them.

One common avenue for recruiting university graduates has always been the job fair, and despite the economy, they continue to be big business. In 2012, for example, San Diego University alone hosted 21 undergraduate job fairs—and that school is just one of the nearly 4,500 degree-granting institutions in the United States. But job fairs aren't nearly effective enough at cutting through the noise that prevents top recruits from finding the best jobs.

L'Oréal, the cosmetics goliath, knew that it needed more qualified job candidates to fill its positions. The company also knew it wanted people with skill sets that weren't on the radar of a high-end makeup brand. From programmers to engineers, the company was hungry for talent but facing difficulty convincing that talent that it wanted *them*.

So in 2010, L'Oréal introduced *Reveal*, a competitive recruitment game (Figure 6.1). The game was directed at graduate students and designed to re-create how candidates might expect their actual working environment to feel. The company's intention was to allow students who might not know where their skill set would be most valuable in the cosmetics industry to experience and better understand everything from product design to marketing and accounting. The game also prompted recruiters to reach out to people achieving the highest scores, thereby matching potentially suitable candidates with job openings.

The game was designed to help students discover a focused career path and also to help that career path discover the students. It provided virtual trial runs through a L'Oréal work environment they would otherwise have to be hired to experience. *Reveal* changed the way L'Oréal recruited by giving people the opportunity to find a deeper understanding about what they want to do—so that when they arrive to do it, they are better suited to the job.

FIGURE 6.1 *L'Oréal Reveal* is a recruitment game designed for university graduates to learn about the cosmetics industry.

Even before the site for the *Reveal* game launched, more than 21,000 people had already signed up to take part with hundreds more throwing in their hats every day, according to TMP Worldwide. It was no wonder that *Reveal* was such a success—L'Oréal had already spent 20 years as a global leader in gamifying recruitment, even before creating *Reveal*. All the way back in 1993 it had launched a real-world competition to assess the skill sets of the company's most serious young recruits and biggest fans. The company called the game *Brandstorm,* and it was designed to not only recruit university students but to recruit them from all over the world.

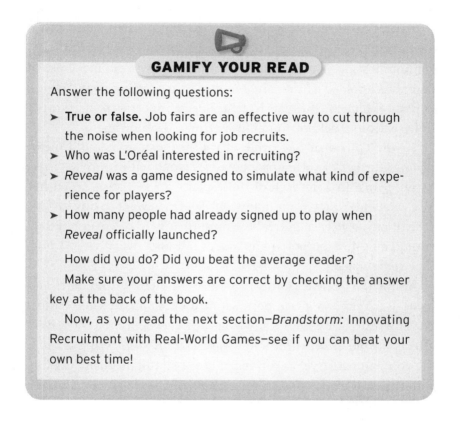

GAMIFY YOUR READ

Answer the following questions:

➤ **True or false.** Job fairs are an effective way to cut through the noise when looking for job recruits.
➤ Who was L'Oréal interested in recruiting?
➤ *Reveal* was a game designed to simulate what kind of experience for players?
➤ How many people had already signed up to play when *Reveal* officially launched?

How did you do? Did you beat the average reader?

Make sure your answers are correct by checking the answer key at the back of the book.

Now, as you read the next section–*Brandstorm:* Innovating Recruitment with Real-World Games–see if you can beat your own best time!

Brandstorm: Innovating Recruitment with Real-World Games

Each year teams of three compete to design and market a new product line for one of L'Oréal's 23 international brands in an international competition called *Brandstorm.* In 2012 teams competed to design products for the Body Shop, a global brand known primarily for its offerings of ethically produced lotions, fragrances, cosmetics, and soaps.

Brandstorm was designed with the intention of creating a forum for the best young minds in marketing to rise to the top. But as a by-product, it gave the company an opportunity to interact with its youngest consumers and better assess their needs and interests. What it learned from them led to some valuable marketing lessons. As part of the 2012 competition, for example, the company asked participants to include possibilities for interactivity with digital communication. The company asked that every team make use of digital technology as a central tenet of its marketing strategy for a hypothetical men's intimate hygiene line. Winners were announced in Paris from a field of competitors from 40 countries.

In the course of one cycle of the *Brandstorm* game, L'Oréal receives dozens of vetted product ideas along with complete marketing plans. In 2012 each of those plans offered ideas about not just what kids today want to buy but *how* they want to buy it. This year *Brandstorm* gave L'Oréal the opportunity to discover not only young, qualified potential employees but also the ways in which they *communicate*.

While the game certainly delivers high-quality candidates and ideas at a very low price point, it also excels in another critical way: it creates a cycle for knowledge and excellence that positively affects the whole organization. Ideas from *Brandstorm* are fed into the company at large, as top recruits are simultaneously learning about the company. Over time, recruitment yields higher-quality candidates. Of particular interest are those with a competitive instinct that respond positively to the challenges presented. The cycle ultimately helps spur the company forward, with L'Oréal VP Sumita Banerjee calling the game "a key pillar of [L'Oréal's] global business strategy."

Design fields have used competition to vet designs and discover talent for years. But using games to recruit can yield surprising results including a better understanding of those hires who are of particular importance in a global market—something that as more and more industries go global is a challenge in and of itself.

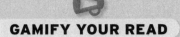

GAMIFY YOUR READ

Answer the following questions:

➤ In 2012 *Brandstorm* focused on new products for what company?

➤ **True or false.** *Brandstorm* recently gave L'Oréal not just the opportunity to find out what kids today will buy but also how they will buy it.

➤ How many countries were represented by teams in the 2012 *Brandstorm* competition?

➤ Of particular interest to L'Oréal are potential recruits with a _____ instinct.

Make sure your answers are correct by checking the answer key at the back of the book.

As you read the next sections in this chapter, continue to clock your time. At the end of the chapter, make sure you post your best score and share your opinions about gamified enterprises by accessing *The Gamification Revolution* app at http:// gamrev.com.

Gamifying an Introduction to Your Employee Base: Marriott Hotels and Domino's Pizza

Using gamification to recruit engineers, technology experts, and other highly skilled candidates is only the tip of the iceberg. Companies seeking unskilled (or less skilled) labor are similarly employing gamified strategies to help build a committed employee base. In fact, even businesses that consider themselves overwhelmed with candidates still have to jump through recruitment hoops in order to find reliable, trustworthy, and hardworking prospective members of their teams.

The hospitality industry is no exception. Food delivery giant Domino's Pizza had long suffered from a famously poor hiring system. Tens of thousands of annual applications were generally ushered into a central location where they languished. The company needed a better way to recruit—and fast—given the importance of service to their value-conscious clientele.

Domino's *Pizza Hero,* a downloadable app, helped the company better connect potential employees to stores with employee vacancies. The app motivates players to virtually knead, top, and bake a pizza in a timely fashion. Other players then vote on the success of the pizza in terms of toppings, appearance, and general hunger-invoking ability. While the game does allow players to order their own or other people's pizza creations, it also scores them. As individuals complete challenges and levels, the company can reach out with job opportunities and incentives for applying.

In the first 28 days, over $1 million worth of pizza was sold through the app, quickly rising to $1 million *per week* after only a few short weeks. And while the recruitment program is still in its infancy, with hundreds of thousands of people using the app each day and a really fun experience at its core, that Domino's job is looking better and better by the minute for thousands of future recruits.

While companies like Domino's can increase their level of depth in an ever-evolving employee search, for companies that struggle with a dearth of employees, a game can prove even more instrumental. Last year, Marriott International, the parent company of the worldwide hotel chain, found itself faced with 50,000 non-U.S. job openings out of a total of 129,000 positions open at any given time. Recruitment outside of the United States, particularly of younger staff, was mostly yielding an underqualified base with high turnover.

Marriott was concerned that the best potential employees were individuals who had not yet considered the hospitality industry as a career. The company launched *My Marriott Hotel* to address what it felt was its branding issue. In some parts of the world, especially China and India where the hotel industry had only just begun to explode, the culture of western business hospitality remained relatively unknown. Moreover, there were few in the potential employee pool who had any previous relevant experience. *My Marriott Hotel* was designed as a game not only to attract a younger generation but also to help bolster the company's image, particularly in places where it could be considered a prestigious career possibility.

First-time players begin by starting a restaurant. Using a model similar to Zynga's popular Facebook game *Farmville* or the casual gaming hit *Diner Dash*, Marriott created a gamified experience where a player does everything from decorating the dining room to ordering the food and maintaining the budget. As they move through the game, the players are able to try out every position within hotel operations.

My Marriott Hotel was offered in multiple languages including English, Mandarin, and Arabic when the game was launched on Facebook in June 2011. Almost immediately, the game attracted tens of thousands of active users and hundreds of thousands of pageviews. One of the most compelling pieces of the *My Marriott Hotel* experience is a banner at the top of the page that reads simply, "Do It For Real." When clicked, it takes you to the list of 50,000 career opportunities as well as to recruiters who can help facilitate the beginning of a conversation.

Training for Meaning

The U.S. Army, L'Oréal, and Marriott all learned that games not only help tease out qualified, interested candidates but also help to deliver a *meaningful* understanding of the positions themselves. As Marriott, for example, expanded into foreign markets, the company immediately encountered a lack of understanding about the products it offered. For example, was a Coke supposed to be served hot or cold? What was the value of that Coke to the customers? Why did they want it? And how could the servers contextualize all of this when a Coke, at least where they came from, frequently cost more than a day's wage?

In an article by Alexandra Guadagno for *Human Resources*, David Kippen, CEO of Evviva, the firm that designed *My Marriott Hotel*, recalled a conversation with a hotel manager in Beijing. The manager, upon hiring a new waiter, said he would watch time and again as each waiter walked to a table, hands shaking, to deliver a glass of Coke.

"His hands are shaking," reports Kippen, "because this stuff is, in a way, liquid gold."

By placing the serving of that Coke into a game context and attaching points to success, Marriott can create incentives and rewards for the correct behavior. For example, servers would see that the Coke is taken out of the refrigerator, poured over ice, and then casually placed on the table in front of the guest. The objective of this cross-cultural teaching and learning is to facilitate under-standing and drive service standards.

While modeling simple behaviors is one thing, using games for more complex challenges, products, or business goals might seem counterintuitive. However, gamification is inspiring a similar depth of comprehension across industries, and they are improving employee performance, knowledge, and as a sidebar, satisfaction.

Knocking Down the Costs of Training

Training has historically been a high-cost arena for many busi-nesses. Sending employees to train at conferences, bringing in lec-turers or trainers to address a specific need, not to mention the cost of time taken from actually getting the job done—all subtract heavily from a business's bottom line.

Some also wonder at the efficacy of many of these training experi-ences for distracted employees who are more interested in exploring the city hosting the conference or who are worried about the missed work back at the office. The employees from generations X and Y as well as the up-and-coming millennials are often disinterested in traditional methods of information dissemination, growing easily distracted if the contact lacks meaning or, to some degree, entertainment value. Plus, how much can people truly take away from a training experience when they are bored, tired, or just don't care?

Training is central to any business. An underprepared staff is taxing on multiple levels. Dropping recent graduates, new recruits, and new hires into the mix can lead to costly production accidents, but in some fields, like healthcare, those mistakes come with a different price tag altogether: life or death.

Since the early 2000s, studies have shown that increased game playing is strongly correlated with improved performance in healthcare. For example, research by Dr. James Rosser of Beth Israel Hospital in New York compared the performance of laparoscopic surgeons based on how much time they spent playing training games. He found that the top one-third of game-playing surgeons made 47 percent fewer errors and were 31 percent faster on a test of their laparoscopic skills called—appropriately—the *Top Gun* test.

But while games have been used successfully in training for decades before Dr. Rosser's work, new social and mobile technologies are being used to deliver early-stage training and development that is lighter weight, more fun, and friendlier than ever before. Blending the lessons of the *Top Gun* test with the preceding examples from Marriott and Domino's, these new games are making amazing inroads. The companies that use gamification believe that they can both filter and train current and prospective employees using game experiences that are proxies for real-world success. Whether it's hard stuff, like *Top Gun,* or relatively easy, like Domino's, the idea that games can really predict success is quite novel and exciting.

Few industries need as much help driving success as hospitals. Although they are an essential part of our healthcare ecosystem, most of them lose money. This happens largely because of the emergency room (ER)—where patients with and without insurance are treated for issues that are generally not fully reimbursed. As healthcare reform expands in the United States and elsewhere, the issue of hospital efficiency becomes ever more critical.

In order to help make hospital management more efficient, General Electric unveiled a virtual interactive experience called

Patient Shuffle in 2010. Long a front-runner in healthcare technology and process, GE designed the game as a way to demonstrate its thought leadership. The game's concept is built on a simple premise: health professionals—including nurses and doctors—don't viscerally understand the challenges of running an emergency room and admissions process from an efficiency perspective.

As teams work in the real world, time to consider the efficiency of their work environment understandably takes a backseat to coping with patient emergencies, during a nonstop, 24-hour patient overload. *Patient Shuffle* offers tools to help doctors and nurses experience the complexity of patient care from admission to discharge. Using a simple concept in the same vein as the hit game *Diner Dash*, with a basic simulation of the ER experience, the game is aimed squarely at reducing the four-hour average time Americans spend waiting to be seen.

However, rather than just playing the game to learn their own piece of the equation (triage, lab services, bedside visits, or something else), the game puts the players into the roles of all-knowing hospital administrators, which ultimately facilitates a meaningful understanding of the roles of coworkers with whom they often interact on a daily basis. The focus is on moving patients through the process, delivering the right care in sequence. As the game advances in complexity, so does the load on the players. Instead of just one patient going from triage to x-ray to doctor visit to discharge, dozens of patients are in every department of the hospital with queues forming for magnetic resonance imaging (MRI) scans and patients requiring more and more tests. In short, it's just like a real hospital—only much more fun.

The game was made for the iPad and iPhone specifically so that practitioners could play it during breaks at or after work. Although some might wonder why professionals would want to play a game about their job during or after work, the trend is well documented—they *are* playing. And it isn't only hospital staff that is playing games that mirror their real-life work. Trends show mothers of small children enjoying virtual baby-nursing games and U.S. Marines maintaining a well-publicized love affair with war games like *Call of Duty* and *Modern Warfare.* Perhaps it's a love of the job or it is simply a comfort zone in which people want to spend more time—whatever the underlying reason, people will play as long as it's *fun.* What these trends show is that games *about* work are growing increasingly popular even after hours.

Happily, this creates a unique opportunity for training an employee population. Instead of isolating training and turning it into a standalone activity outside of work, gamification unlocks a whole new modality: training as continuous recreation. Provided that the games are easy to understand, engaging, and mobile, there is no limit to the amount of time doctors might play a medical game, lawyers might play a legal game, or chefs might play a cooking game. Organizations and industries that leverage this trend should see a significant boost in engagement and outcomes as total training time could equal or exceed actual working time.

Training Games: *Rise of the Shadow Specters*

A 2010 study by the University of Denver Business School revealed that organizations utilizing video games in their training systems end up with an employee base that is not only more motivated but that also shows marked increases in levels of retention over the long term. Using 65 studies and 6,476 trainees, the researchers found that those employees who had used video games in their training had 11 percent more factual knowledge and 14 percent more skill-based knowledge than those who did not use video games. In addition, their rate of retention was 9 percent higher.

The study further revealed that the *kind* of games offered made a difference in the effectiveness of their outcomes. In other words, not all games make useful training tools. Video games, with their requirement for active participation, are more efficient and better performers across the board than alternatives.

In 2007, the technology company Sun Microsystems rolled out two active training tools for new hires called *Rise of the Shadow Specters* and *Dawn of the Shadow Specters.* The tech company set play in an alternate universe they call "Solaris." Solaris is divided into five worlds representing the five business units within the company. Using the company's core values to drive play, players must utilize the various products or company philosophies to save the respective worlds from the "shadow specters."

Sun Microsystems had three major obstacles it meant to overcome through the game:

1. Its employee base mostly worked remotely, which created a sense of isolation for many of them.
2. It needed an engaging way to train employees as well as to better explain the brand.
3. Sun Microsystems was struggling with something of an image issue. With an aging workforce averaging 45 years (considered "old" by tech industry standards), it was largely interested in attracting young recruits.

The adventure game offers a series of exciting challenges—such as avoiding evil attackers, opening locked doors, and finding lost objects essential for the team to function. In each case, the solution to the challenge is an element of the company's mission, values, or vision. Although answers to many of the specific questions are fairly obvious, the game is nonetheless engaging enough that anyone would want to spend an hour (or more) with it—something we did on multiple occasions—you know... for research.

Despite fanciful names and descriptions that come right out of a Hollywood plot, *Rise* and *Dawn of the Shadow Specters* are accom-

Play *Rise of the Shadow Specters* by downloading *The Gamification Revolution* app at http://gamrev.com.

plishing an important and valuable end result. Each has met three out of three of its goals. Players feel greater alignment with the company. They have reported the retention of "a decent amount of high-level information" about the brand, according to a publicized follow-up assessment. Almost all of the players agreed that they would be confident having a conversation about Sun Microsystems as a brand and as a culture, and they felt they could convey what the company did. But most important, buzz about the game spread far and wide, attracting the broader base of potential recruits that the company so desperately sought.

The Four-Door Approach to Learning: Using Choice in Play

Using gamification to help your employee base train as well as to stay ahead of the latest trends can lead to a happier and better engaged workforce. By engaging them, they will be better informed about your brand and products, more adept at understanding and conveying your brand's goals, and more successful as brand representatives both inside and outside of your company community.

However, blindly adding games to just any training experience promises to accomplish *none of those things* if the games aren't nuanced to fit the items being taught. Additionally, they should be taught in the way they are best learned by the people to whom they are being conveyed. Dr. Sivasailam "Thiagi" Thiagarajan, the self-proclaimed "mad scientist" at the Thiagi Group, works with corporations from AT&T to Chevron to "help people improve their performance effectively and enjoyably." He developed something he calls the Four-Doors Approach to e-Learning. This system has been broadly adopted in successful gamified training—whether intentional or not—and can be seen in many of the apps described in this chapter.

The system offers users four options as users approach a new learning experience:

- *The library.* Here users will find all the information they need to master the training. It includes data, videos, documents, and any other preexisting collected materials that the users can peruse and take in at whatever pace they choose.
- *The playground.* Games in this section should be fast-paced, and they should help users lock in the requisite information. Generally offered at three levels of difficulty, users can play as often or as many times as they want to improve their understanding.
- *The cafe.* Here's where the training experiences become social. Games allow users to compare their answers with those of peers and experts. The games also include spaces for compiling additional information in the style of Wikipedia and blogs.
- *The evaluation torture chamber.* These games are the actual test components of the experience, and they can include actual real-world, work-related components and/or a series of questions that tests for understanding and knowledge.

What the Four-Door Approach offers the users is something very valuable when it comes to an educational experience: choice. Having a sense of agency while learning allows individuals the opportunity to learn at their own pace, in their own style, and to greater efficacy. People can spend more time on items that confuse them. They can work slowly or speed along. But more important, they can work in a way that is meaningful for them. All these things will take their training from being perfunctory to being their own choice—a better way to learn.

Gamifying the Learning Process

A young recruit, formerly a classics major at a liberal arts college, takes a job as a sales rep for a pharmaceutical company. She's more familiar with Dionysus than Diovan, more familiar with Ajax than Avonex. Now suddenly she has to be able to differentiate between a complicated list of prescription drugs and their active ingredients.

Training employees can sometimes be as difficult as recruiting them in the first place. Forcing people to sit through long-winded PowerPoint presentations or boring industrial videos will at best loosely explain complicated products and campaigns. At worst, they will give your new employees a crick in the neck. But other than going home and memorizing note cards, the knowledge that your young classics major is going to retain is what she will acquire when she's already out in the field, when she should *already know* what she's selling.

That is why in 2007 Daiichi Sankyo, a Japanese pharmaceutical company, created a *critter-killing game.* As the company was getting ready to repurpose a cholesterol drug to sell as a treatment for type 2 diabetes, there was a lot of high science to impart to a relatively young sales force. Rather than hand over folders filled with reading material, the company built a game. Every time employees used their robot avatar to kill a series of pesky animals, they were presented with a fact about the drug. Game users could then exchange that knowledge for points, better weaponry, and to complete in-game tasks.

High-tech companies, with their ever-changing products and methods, are already modeling a need for project-by-project training methods. Social and mobile-savvy hires tend to be well ahead of the curve, having already engaged with products, brands, and market research before starting a new job and having already used advanced tools. But as businesses across industries become more fluid and grow ever more complex, an ongoing training system might prove the best way to keep staff engaged and in the know from day one to retirement.

According to a follow-up by BrandGames, Daiichi Sankyo reported that their staff found the game to be a useful training tool with players deeming it a fun way to learn. The company reported that their reps were able to successfully disseminate difficult concepts including the high-science and clinical aspects of

Training for Peripheral Knowledge

When I took my first job out of graduate school, it was with net-working giant Cisco. The role I played kept me far from the routers and switches that powered the Internet for which the company was known. During discussions with various managers about the under-lying technology, I was routinely given the runaround, being told that such knowledge "wasn't necessary" or that it was "beyond a mere mortal's scope of comprehension."

While the company certainly has an excellent track record of success, the boundary I repeatedly found myself up against high-lights one of the risks of overspecialization. In fact, some degree of technical literacy for all its employees would very likely have ben-efited Cisco across the board. Now, as new gamification approaches extend the reach of science, nonspecialized employees can gain surer footing in the key elements of any company's key operation, creating strong brand alignment and the possibility for advocacy among employees at every level and in every corner. With a team like that, the possibilities are endless.

—Gabe Zichermann

the medication. Initially the game didn't promise prizes. But as it steadily grew in success, company leaders began offering prizes to high scorers, quickly prompting even more interest in the program and ultimately a better trained staff. In fact, when the next drug was released—Prasugrel for acute coronary syndrome—so too was a follow-up training game.

Using Simulations to Train with Gamification

Most people have some memory of their schools taking a break from the daily chore of education in order to take part in a color war or field day. Other people probably recall a lazy afternoon game of hangman at the end of English class or a tag team race to solve equations in math. Most of us probably wished those could have been more the rule of the day and less the exception to it.

It's safe to assume most of us would rather play an entertaining game to learn than be force-fed data in almost any other way. The Defense Acquisitions University trains military and civilian Department of Defense personnel in the fields of acquisition, technology, and logistics. The *Procurement Fraud Indicators Game* was developed in order to teach employees to spot fraud (Figure 6.2). Rather than simply listing the warning signs of fraudulent behavior for an individual to memorize, the game actually facilitates *practice*, virtual though it may be. The game places the players as fraud investigators in a point-and-click environment. Players are able to choose among seven different fraud scenarios and investigate each one. Each scenario takes players through a variety of scenes in which they can investigate fraudulent behavior, gather evidence,

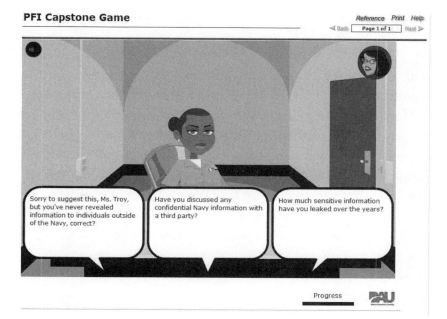

FIGURE 6.2 The *Procurement Fraud Indicators Game* allows players to form hypotheses about a crime during an extensive fraud investigation.

interview suspects, and make conclusions about the committed fraud. Winning the game involves gathering the right clues and pursuing the correct theory about each suspect.

As with any subjective skill, experience and expertise are closely related—practice, you could say, falls just a step below real-world experience. Imagine if the first time a firefighter saw a fire, your home was the one engulfed in flames. That's why firefighters who train actually fight "real" fires first—staged though they may be. But imagine the alternative: reading a list in front of a roomful of trainees of the ways to fight the fire—or in the case of the Department of Defense, the warning signs of fraudulent behavior. Such an exercise would probably fall somewhere well below "practice" in terms of conveying useful information, and it would be perhaps only slightly more meaningful than watching some TV show like *Rescue Me* (about firefighters) or *CSI* (about solving crimes) and calling it "training." The bottom line is that doing will always outperform reading as a way of skills acquisition, and gamification presents the best way to foster doing in a scalable way.

Although it has a long and storied history, the contemporary use of gamification in recruitment, training, and development is growing rapidly, easily outpacing old-fashioned methodologies. In fields as disparate as hospitality, medicine, food service, and technology, as well as the hundreds of start-ups in between, companies are acquiring talent and driving better performance through games. But human performance isn't a purely intellectual pursuit. As we'll see in the next chapter, organizations are including employee health and wellness in their human capital strategy. Gamification is having an outsized effect in that vertical too—lowering absenteeism and healthcare costs, improving satisfaction, and ultimately driving performance.

7

PROPELLING PERSONNEL TO HEALTH AND WELLNESS

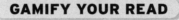

Here's a counterintuitive idea: higher status can actually make us healthier.

While most people logically believe that the pressures of having more people dependent on us and more people with expectations of us might actually make the opposite true, studies are proving that the perks of high status outweigh its disadvantages—statistically adding years to your life.

The most compelling of this evidence began to take form in 1985, when a group of British scientists began a long-term study of workers at the British Civil Service—the legal branch of the government of the United Kingdom. Known as the *Whitehall Study*, it took an in-depth look at the health of more than 10,000 women and men between the ages of 35 and 55. Researchers wanted to study the general health of a workforce made up of individuals from similar socioeconomic, ethnic, and educational backgrounds. Most of the subjects were lawyers or had legal backgrounds; however, the experimental control of the study was unique in that subjects worked in the same physical environment with perfectly equal access to healthcare along with a consistent status system that filtered across the organization. Much like the military, the British Civil Service is divided into organizations that are then subdivided by grade and rank.

Given this exceptional consistency, and armed with each employee's long-term rank and health history, researchers asked one simple question: How does status affect health and mortality in humans? From its earliest stages, the *Whitehall Study* showed that individuals employed in positions with higher status *lived longer* than those employed in lower spheres. Upon looking more closely, it revealed that the deaths of those lower-ranking individuals were largely due to heart disease that could be traced to a significant increase in the following risk factors: obesity, smoking, high blood pressure, and long work hours. Because the research normalized the backgrounds of participants, the results were startlingly clear: low status at the office was literally killing employees.

A follow-up study 20 years later called *Whitehall II* enlisted the same participants to dig even deeper into the first-round results. What they found was shocking. By accounting for even more external data, researchers discovered that workplace factors—including rank and status—were even more significant predictors of health and wellness than things like fitness, smoking, and eating habits.

In other words, low-status employees *despite an otherwise healthy lifestyle* exhibited an increased risk of symptoms of stress-induced wear and tear on their bodies.

In another compelling study, a Stanford University professor, Robert Sapolsky, asked a similar question of baboon culture. After years of careful study in the Kenyan wild, what he discovered was that *higher-status primates had lower overall stress.* A Princeton University researcher, Laurence R. Gesquiere, corroborated Sapolsky's claim. She proved that overall, high-ranking male baboons are lower in stress hormones than their lower-ranking counterparts during times of danger.

We are not baboons. However, our level of responsibility in the workplace and, more specifically, our social standing among our colleagues, can shorten or lengthen our lives. On a day-to-day level, it certainly influences our health: higher stress levels having been linked to lower-functioning immune systems. Over the long term, it profoundly shapes the culture, productivity, and reliability of a workforce, not to mention a society as a whole.

The answer to the question of "why" higher ranking equals lower stress remains speculative. Perhaps those in higher ranked positions have less to worry about in terms of the minutiae of the daily grind. Or maybe it's that the drive for higher status—for those who have not yet achieved it—stresses people out in a persistent and insidious way. One thing is certain: the effects of status—both positive and negative—have a direct cost and impact on the success of business.

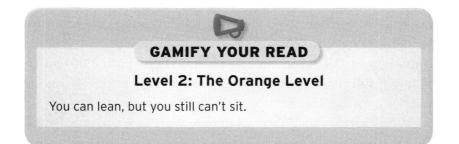

GAMIFY YOUR READ

Level 2: The Orange Level

You can lean, but you still can't sit.

But while it might be difficult to earn status readily in the real world, there is one place where gaining status is within everyone's grasp—and that's in the world of games. Proof is rapidly coming to the forefront indicating that along with the pleasure people feel as they level up and accrue status in a gaming environment there is a correlated decrease in their stress levels. As a result, they tend to be happier and better adjusted in other aspects of their life—including their work life. It's like everybody wins!

And it's a good thing too because the alternative offers some fairly bleak numbers: in the United States, Gallup estimates that over $153 billion in productivity was lost from preventable illness and poor wellness in 2011 alone, with stress proving a leading cause of decreased immune system function. "Presenteeism"—or going to work while you're sick—cost U.S. employers $180 billion in a similar time frame. And these crazy numbers don't even include the upside: workers who are healthy and fit demonstrate improved cognitive performance and ultimately increased contribution to the bottom line.

Fundamentally, it's in our best interest from a health and wellness standpoint to deal with stress first and foremost in our quest for healthier living. In fact, we could argue that the biggest public health intervention we can make is to reduce modern stress levels. If we did, people would very likely eat better, sleep better, and experience fewer reproductive and digestive interruptions. They would be healthier overall.

While much of the discussion on healthcare reform has centered around the new cost to businesses of providing insurance-related products, industry already bears a huge burden for poor employee health. And while we can't pin the accelerating costs of healthcare on status alone, we also can't ignore the problem. However, creating status opportunities for everyone just won't prove a viable solution to this health crisis. But smart organizations have begun leveraging the power of gamification to create healthier workforces.

Whether they focus on stress reduction or positive behavior change, this chapter's examples help contextualize and inspire different ways of thinking about and affecting change in the health and wellness of our employees.

People are status driven and status oriented. The *Whitehall Study* illustrates that status has a direct effect on stress. Stress-related diseases are believed by experts to account for up to 80 percent of all doctor visits in the United States. Because it seems we are biologically wired to seek status, status makes us healthier, and as these studies have shown, status is highly predictive of health. Meanwhile, games are one of the best ways to bolster a sense of accomplishment and visibly elevated status among individuals.

So you see where we are going here: companies of all sizes can leverage this reality to improve the health (and lives) of their employees. There are two basic ways we can accomplish this: by using "good stress" to balance "bad stress" while creating new ways for our employees to "level up."

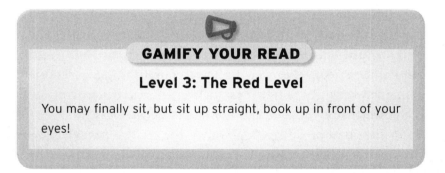

GAMIFY YOUR READ

Level 3: The Red Level

You may finally sit, but sit up straight, book up in front of your eyes!

Eustress and Dopamine

Eustress is a word commonly used to describe "good stress," or the opposite of distress. Imagine the feeling of soaring over the big hill on a roller coaster or the butterflies-in-your-stomach rush associated with a passionate kiss. Both of those sensations are versions of eustress.

This positive stress is common during game play. In theory, eustress comes about when a player is exploring the potential gains associated with what can be accomplished or won in a state of play. Unlike bad stress, eustress is actually good for the body. After a burst of it, the body settles rapidly back to stasis, much like a healthy fight-or-flight response in animals in the wild. Eustress also seems to actually motivate learning, growth, excitement, and achievement. Where its evil twin "stress" manages to carry out the opposite: a breaking down, a rendering of inactivity, and even an increase in discomforts—such as anxiety and fear.

Some studies are beginning to show that eustress occurs any time people know they are in a system in which achievement (or some similar reward system) is possible—as in a game. If people have been positively reinforced that succeeding, compounding successes, or even ultimately winning is within their capability, they will begin to experience eustress.

Because eustress occurs naturally in most good gamified design, implementing a game-based approach within your organization can confer the health benefits of eustress on your company's players. Care should certainly be taken to design an experience with a healthful arc, one that particularly allows users to become stressed but then immediately relaxed after accomplishing a goal. When combined with a system that can deliver enhanced status, eustress is a powerful ally in your fight for employee wellness.

In classic game design, a player in the *eustress behavioral loop* works toward achievable challenges that result in success, which releases dopamine that, in turn, returns you to the challenge loop. This can occur in high-stakes games like *Diablo 3* where one mistake costs players greatly, more average-challenge games like *Temple Run*, or in relaxed modes, such as in the most casual games like *Tetris* or *Farmville*.

The dopamine release loop is what happens in our brains when something is achieved (Figure 7.1). The neurotransmitter dopamine is known to encourage a number of positive behaviors including relaxation. Even more, it encourages us to want more of it by activating its five known receptors. While this is arguably true for all neurotransmitters, in the case of dopamine, it is particularly true.

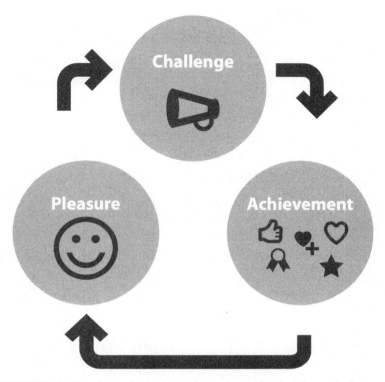

FIGURE 7.1 In the *dopamine release loop*, dopamine is released when people challenge themselves to something and then achieve that objective. This causes pleasure and a desire to do the loop again.

It is in large part because of this characteristic of dopamine that human beings are hardwired evolutionarily to seek challenges and overcome them. What's uniquely interesting about games and the positive eustress loops they create is that all it takes to trigger one is a single engaging challenge that anyone can overcome. In turn, this will drive our desire to get that dopamine again.

While less challenge might seem the logical way to decrease stress for your employees, it seems that the opposite is also true: to improve employee health and wellness *increase* challenges to also potentially increase eustress, and thereby improve job satisfaction and performance. It turns out that companies have been doing this for a very long time. The corporate softball tournament is one example of a great case study of a eustress-promoting activity for team building, camaraderie, stress reduction, and blowing off steam. But what if, instead of making that a side event once a month, it was part of the whole organization—at every level and in every activity?

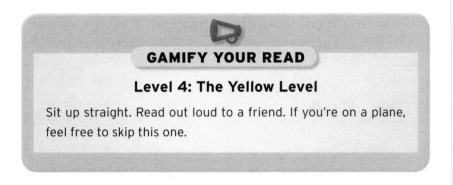

GAMIFY YOUR READ

Level 4: The Yellow Level

Sit up straight. Read out loud to a friend. If you're on a plane, feel free to skip this one.

World of *Work*craft: Reducing Stress

Every day, 11 million people log on to play the massively multiplayer online role-playing game (MMORPG) *World of Warcraft*. In their day-to-day lives they might be delivery people, students, doctors, or librarians, but after work they become healers or "tanks" doing battle for a common goal.

Ask any one of those 11 million players what they'd rather be doing—their day job or playing their game—and it's safe to assume that few would choose their day job. Of course, we'd never suggest that you re-create your business strategy using a fanciful world inhabited by monsters and medieval princes unless you own a theme park. However, we do suggest you consider some of its most basic tools. After all, *World of Warcraft*, or WoW as it is called by its many fanatical fans, is one of the most popular games ever built. It is so popular, in fact, that websites and support groups exist in droves for its players' so-called widows.

Of particular importance to a chapter about basic health and wellness is the idea that players of this game are able to achieve a certain amount of self-satisfaction and self-worth by acquiring more gear, raising their experience, and interacting with peers and friends. As their satisfaction levels visibly rise, their stress levels have been shown to markedly decrease.

In fact, a 2009 study conducted at the Queensland University of Technology surveyed 200 *World of Warcraft* players who were considered to maintain a healthy balance between their virtual and real life. It concluded that the social value of working together in a team, or in the vernacular of WoW, a "guild," actually provided people with a sense of belonging. Anxiety, depression, and stress all decreased.

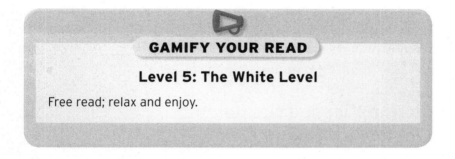

GAMIFY YOUR READ

Level 5: The White Level

Free read; relax and enjoy.

Most workplaces include some sort of inherent hierarchical leveling system, as we've mentioned. There are managers, workers, and new employees as well as pay-grade levels in constant rotation. The *Whitehall* and baboon studies might imply that if businesses simply promote every employee to manager—Boom! Our problems would be solved: less stress, better health! However, such a move would be impractical at best, and it would be tactically difficult—if not impossible—to execute.

By offering opportunities for your employees to level up in gamified experiences, you can bring about that same feeling of self-satisfaction and self-worth they experience in games. For example, encourage employees to play various MMORPGs throughout the workweek as a benefit for a job well done. Suggest they play with other colleagues; then record and display their team scores for everyone in the office to see. Or take workaday tasks and gamify them—like awarding points and achievements for recycling or being on telephone duty—and give employees the opportunity to run guilds battling office-related problems. Make sure they receive acknowledgment for it.

Although it may be hard to achieve increased status for all employees through mechanics like titles and ranks, there is an almost limitless sandbox of ways to offer status through gamification. Ultimately, it can help to improve energy, reduce stress, and increase wellness in general. Some great examples of this concept at work are the projects of Nextjump, a profitable e-commerce company focused on building loyalty and incentive programs for employee and customer groups. They have 100 million users and 84 percent of the Fortune 100 as strategic partners. And now Nextjump is proving that gamification can change your employees—and your company output—from the inside out.

Charlie Kim and Nextjump's Employee Workout Game

To Nextjump CEO and founder Charlie Kim, wanting his employee base to exercise is both a personal passion and good business. As healthcare costs began to spiral out of control for the company, the addition of expensive in-office gyms proved worthless. With a staff made up primarily of engineers, software developers, and web designers, its employee base was remarkably sedentary as a population. So the company did something revolutionary: it turned working out into a game (Figure 7.2).

Nextjump divided its workforce into teams mixing regular gym users with nongym users. Then it established a leaderboard ranking the teams based on their collective workout prowess. Eventually the company had motivated an average of 50 percent of its employees to work out two times a week. The number was good, but not good enough. As management saw users reach a plateau, they stepped up the game.

FIGURE 7.2 Nextjump's fitness portal encourages employees to work out to receive different gamified benefits.

GAMIFY YOUR READ

Level 6: The Green Level

Stand up and sit down between every paragraph. Think of it as exercise!

The company already had a system in place offering steady awards, badges, and prizes to reward employees for any number of work-related behaviors. When one of the teams achieved the impossible by motivating 100 percent of its team members to work out one week, Kim publicly rewarded that team leader with a substantial bonus in his paycheck as well as public recognition for the achievement.

The team leader, unprompted, used his bonus to buy T-shirts for his team, further propagating that sense of accomplishment. Soon,

80 percent of Nextjump's employees were working out regularly. Put into perspective, most gyms and clubs whose members pay to join expect only 33 percent of them to use their memberships *once a year*, according to Club Industry statistics. In effect, Nextjump has a 300 percent performance advantage over a health club where members pay for the privilege of—it would seem—*not going*.

The Surprise Results

Nextjump did manage to lower its healthcare overhead, but that wasn't the only benefit the company was afforded.

Kim realized early on that by motivating his employee base to get healthier, he was inspiring them to have a better life. He explained that he began to see health as the top and bottom pieces of a pyramid. The lower half symbolizes physical health, which he believes has its base in exercise—which, in turn, promotes healthy eating habits and better sleeping patterns. The top half of the pyramid, according to Kim, is an individual's mental health. Nextjump provides enrichment programs for its employees such as a program they call Nextjump University. But at the core of the mental health piece of the pyramid Kim also sees exercise.

The Nextjump fitness promotion continues to evolve in order to maintain momentum and look for ways to motivate those employees who have not yet started playing the game. But in the meantime Nextjump has seen improvements in its teams' performance during their working hours as well as an increase in the speed at which they work.

Every year the company sends its staff of 150 engineers in teams of three to charitable causes for two weeks to code on their behalf. These outside sources report back that Nextjump employees outpace and outperform everyone else they work with, every time.

"I see a strong correlation between their health and what they are able to accomplish in short periods," Kim said. "The things we have done to motivate our employees to exercise has enabled them to do more faster."

Similarly, in an industry like technology where skilled employees are in demand, Nextjump's employee turnover is well below average, loyalty is extraordinary, and employee satisfaction is high. It is the company's belief that if you can engage and motivate your employees to improve their health and wellness, you are ultimately building a business that is healthy and strong.

To be sure, some of this success is due to Kim's personality and the organization's overall "winning" attitude. But after all this time, it's tough to tell where one begins and the other ends. Critically, Kim implemented the system with an opt-in approach. Where other companies have tried to compel employees to be healthier through penalties or strict hiring rules, Nextjump does it by building experiences that employees want to engage in.

The Nextjump example points out the benefits of a long-term and highly successful employee health and wellness game. And encouraging staff to improve their physical health over the long term is a smart way to go if you can do it. However, businesses that aren't ready to build in-house gyms or create complex gamified strategies around getting their employees to use them might consider smaller-scale options. For example, what if your employees could expect a once-a-day inbox message telling them to stop what they are doing and go for a 10-minute walk? The next day the message might suggest that they stop and drink a full glass of water or call their spouse, parent, or child to say hello. Over time, people who took the action suggested in the daily e-mail might be issued stars on a leaderboard for their daily accomplishment. Those stars could then be traded in for a "casual Friday" or a free morning yoga class.

Perhaps tellingly, Kim has suggested that building a motivated and healthy employee base should supersede the development of your consumer base. After all, he says, "If you won't eat it yourself, don't feed it to your guests."

Charlie Kim is an incredibly inspiring guy—and you can devour tons more information about him and his radical management style at Nextjump by downloading *The Gamification Revolution* app at http://gamrev.com to start interacting with colleagues and taking notes through the power of games.

GAMIFY YOUR READ

Level 7: The Purple Level

Read this section, and then take a walk to the closest purple object you can find. Once you're there, touch it, turn around, and come back.

Stress Test

Which would be harder: getting employees into good physical shape to increase their energy and therefore their output, or stress them into working harder with threats, demotions, and pay cuts? Unfortunately, for short-term results, the latter seems very likely your best bet, no matter how negative its long-term effects.

However, Adam Bosworth, Google Health founder and CEO of gamified employee wellness start-up Keas, disagrees. In fact, his data indicates that the more positively you reward people for getting into shape, the easier it is for them to actually get into shape. He should know: Keas specializes in delivering employee wellness programs based on gamification principles to hundreds of blue-chip companies.

Bosworth also stresses another key concept: the power of points. In a revealing discussion, he indicated that the point system used by Keas to track employee behavior was the most important thing to end users in the system: "I never would have thought that the number one thing our [employee incentives] cus-tomers would want to talk about—positively and negatively—was

Healthy Apps

Keas	*Nike+*	*Endomondo*
Work.com	*Zamzee* (kids)	*Sports-Tracker*
Earndit	*Fitbit*	

points." It seems that the success of Keas is proof of the power of points to drive healthy employee behavior, though the site does use a wide range of game mechanics in its design.

The basic concept in the Keas design is that employees form teams designed to motivate each other to achieve health and wellness objectives. Through completing a range of tasks—both action and motivation oriented—teams earn points, virtual and physical rewards, as well as recognition. The company claims that over 90 percent of players say they would recommend the service to a friend, with over 70 percent actively engaged with it.

As the Keas systems illustrate, there are simple everyday ways to encourage employees to lower stress, increase their fitness habits, and improve their diets. Using any of the apps and programs already available—see box "Healthy Apps"—you can motivate your employees without having to design a brand-new gamified experience.

In a world where social networks are used by billions of people, getting users into a positive feedback loop is simpler than ever. And many health games, apps, and gamified programs use systems with which your workforce is very likely already familiar. If you don't want to do it yourself, the gamified programs can add tools designed to remind employees to take a minute to stretch or encouraging that 10-minute power walk around the building. They can even teach people to eat right and enjoy getting healthier. All of these things take on increasing importance in the context of rising healthcare costs, illness, and time spent at work.

The Biggest Loser

In October 2004, NBC premiered a new reality TV show called *The Biggest Loser* that featured a group of obese contestants competing to lose the most weight for a cash prize. A contestant named Ryan Benson originally weighed in at 330 pounds. The Spokane, Washington, resident had never had much luck battling his weight. However, during the competition, Benson lost a staggering 122 pounds in roughly three months—or the length of the season—and became the first winner. The show was a hit, and 11 subsequent seasons followed.

How was it that Benson, a person of at least reasonable intelligence who had, by his own admission, struggled with weight loss for much of his 36 years of life—and after appearing on the show, gained every pound back—suddenly, in a burst of extreme dieting and exercise, managed to shed more than one-third of his body weight in under four months?

The easy answer is games. But let's make no mistake: it isn't just any game. For a greyhound to run a track, a bunny dangled in front of him on a string might be the only "game mechanic," or motivator, that you need to get him to run his fastest. However, for those of us with two legs and a lot of sedentary entertainment possibilities, getting us to run a track is going to take a whole lot more than a synthetic rabbit.

The Biggest Loser is a comprehensive weight loss game that leverages prizes, leaderboards, point systems, and perhaps most important, status in order to compel its players to lose the highest percentage of weight possible in an 11- to 21-week period. The TV show affords a monetary six-figure grand prize, but obviously the biggest motivator is status on a national level. While most businesses can't afford six-figure prizes, they can offer some level of status and certainly bragging rights.

Biggest Loser challenges are becoming more and more common in offices around the country. They are a good way to promote health and wellness over a period of time. What's important to note is that the short-term results of these games speak for themselves

Visit *The Gamification Revolution* app at http://gamrev.com to find resources and more information for gamifying your employee wellness, including a quick list of URLs and Twitter handles for all the companies mentioned here.

in terms of the power of game mechanics to motivate not just weight loss but dramatic lifestyle changes. Even in Europe, where weight loss has historically been less of a concern, companies offer incentives for worker participation in team sports and small fitness activities like *step challenges* where staff count and compare their overall movement.

The Pitfalls of Motivating Health and Wellness

Unfortunately, games like *The Biggest Loser* don't always create lifestyle changes that stick. Further, they are often linked to unhealthy behaviors including dehydrating the body before weigh-ins and other starvation practices.

Charlie Kim has admitted that Nextjump made some fairly poor choices at times while trying to figure out the best ways to motivate his employees to work out. At one point the company attempted to push individuals making the least amount of effort to go to the gym into a fitness regimen. Using peer pressure to drive motivation, the company implemented a game it now admits lacked sensitivity (even referring to it as "Fishing for Whales"). Teams were encouraged to get teammates who refused to work out into the gym or they wouldn't be eligible to win the weekly prize. After what practically amounted to bullying tactics, it was put to a stop. To combat this and even out the teams, the company developed its own *FitRank*—a score measuring health and wellness for individuals. It then used this score to create more balanced teams and make the experience fairer.

By taking note of the impact your games are having, you can control the way your employees respond to them. Focused tactics like encouraging people to race toward specific weight loss and workout goals—rather than a weight loss/workout free-for-all—can help you avoid team members taking things too far. For example, instead of challenging your employees to lose as much weight as they can in a period of time in the spirit of the TV game show, have them each write out how much they'd like to lose in a period of time. The person who comes the closest **without going over** wins. Clearly, this demonstrates one of the best aspects of gamification techniques for health and wellness: they can be low tech, cheap, and quick to implement and maintain. All you need is a bulletin board or a shared Google doc.

GAMIFY YOUR READ

Level 8: The Gold Level

Get yourself a beverage (we recommend a crisp Pilsner) and a snack! You have reached the highest level, and you deserve it. As you read this section, be good to yourself and bask in the glow of your accomplishment!

All's Well That Ends Well

There are many ways to weave games into your business to promote health and wellness. You can make optional, gamified exercise a part of your corporate culture, as Nextjump has done, eventually even redesigning your organization around it. Or you can incentivize from the outside, as Keas has done, using one of a dozen available apps. Or you can incorporate *Biggest Loser* challenges to drive specific wellness goals. Regardless of what you do, gamifying health and wellness provides nearly limitless benefits to your organization's cohesion, employee satisfaction, and performance.

But in terms of the employee experience, gamification is having a profound effect on its every aspect. Human capital managers are incorporating the perks of games into all aspects of employee recruitment, retention, training, and development, and in so doing they are creating workplaces where people actually want to go to work! While every company has its own unique resources, approaches, and cultures, the fundamentals of leveraging *feedback*, *friends*, and *fun* to drive engagement are universal.

It goes without saying that the happiness of your employees will benefit your customers. In fact, the only thing your customers might begin to wonder is this: Why not them? And frankly, why *not* them? Gamification can promise just as much long-term engagement and satisfaction when applied to your customers—using the same three Fs you use to motivate your staff. While customers may not respond to edicts and cash incentives quite the same way as employees, they nonetheless are looking for meaningful, durable, and dynamic relationships with the brands they trust. Lessons learned in the employee sphere can also be applied to consumers—and the examples they offer show no less inspiring results. Let's look more closely at the other side of *The Gamification Revolution*—your customer—and see where we can find the patterns that bring all of these strategies together.

PART III

CONNECTING, ENGAGING, AND LEVERAGING YOUR CUSTOMER BASE

8

CUTTING THROUGH
THE CONSUMER NOISE

★

Around the turn of the millennium, a new app was launched. Its purpose was poetic yet simple: make it easier than ever to actually connect with your friends while you and they are out and about. Dodgeball, at its launch, was one of about two dozen *location-based systems* (LBSs), but it rapidly became the most popular, earning it a reputation as one of the first "hipster" apps of this

---

📢

GAMIFY YOUR READ

Point Game: Follow Your Dreams!

Imagine your ideal customers. Do you know individual customers by name? How old are they? Go ahead and give them a few other characteristics until they are clear in your mind. As you read the chapter, answer the questions marked "Gamify Your Read." Every one you can answer earns a point, every blank gets nothing. If at the end of the chapter you have 5 points or more, your business is primed and ready to **snag the customers of your dreams!**

---

era. Using their computers and mobile phones, via SMS technology, users "checked in," indicating their presence at various locations. By using the application, users appeared on a list that indicated their mutual presence. In this way, you might bump into friends and contacts simply by way of having been alerted to their presence in a particular place. Essentially, the app let you know how near or far you were to a serendipitous encounter by listing the real-time locations of your friends and contacts.

The idea at first seemed brilliant. People would simply show up, check in, and wait for their friends to come out and meet them. In terms of its marketing possibilities, the idea was remarkable—so much so that it was acquired by Google in 2005 for a rumored $2.5 million. Not bad for a student project that was only a few months old.

What Dodgeball's founders, Dennis Crowley and Naveen Selvadurai, couldn't anticipate was the possibility that once the novelty wore off, people would stop checking in. It turned out that Dodgeball wasn't easier than just texting your friends where you were—and it was much less accurate. For example, what if your friend checked in on her way to another venue but didn't then let you know when she left? What if your ex was out on a date and didn't want you to know about it? But even more important than those questions was the simplest of all: What if users stopped caring about checking in?

Over time they did. As the popularity of the app faded, so too did Crowley and Selvadurai's and Google's—interest. The founders left in 2007, and the service was shut down in 2009. However, through Dodgeball they had seen the light, and just after their Google lockup ended, Crowley and Selvadurai launched a brand-new LBS. The new product was striking in similarity to the original concept, but there was one key difference—and this small change would revolutionize not only the nascent location services industry but soon marketing as a whole: they added gamification.

By incentivizing the behavior of the check-in, the app went from inspiring serendipity to creating a frenzy. Foursquare, as Dodgeball

2 would be known, was launched in 2009 to much fanfare (Figure 8.1). The new system quantified each check-in, showing the users' progress at discovering the world around them. Also, to give the check-in even more depth of meaning, Foursquare began issuing badges based on behavior. The hilarious, attractive, surprising, and/or limited-edition badges have over the years included these:

> The Player Please badge awarded for checking in someplace with three or more members of the opposite sex
> The School Night badge for checking in after 3 a.m. on a weekday
> The Last Degree badge awarded in April 2012 to Parker Liautaud, 15, and David Newman, 44, for being the first people to use *Foursquare* to check in to the North Pole

You can check out a wide range of Foursquare badges and other great examples of how to focus consumer attention with gamification on *The Gamification Revolution* social app that you can access at http://gamrev.com.

Users also became able to reap status benefits by becoming regulars at certain establishments. Enough check-ins on their mobile devices could earn them the title of "mayor." Over time, establishments themselves started offering users rewards to those who achieved the honor, like a free

FIGURE 8.1 Foursquare, a location-based game, allows users, through check-ins, to unlock badges and work toward becoming the mayor.

drink or VIP service. A 2010 article in the *New York Times,* "Who Elected Me Mayor? I Did," suggested the Foursquare mayorship had taken on a life of its own. Users were playfully fighting over the rights to the title everywhere from their favorite coffee shops to their offices as well as their entire neighborhoods.

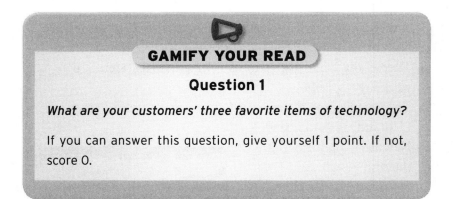

GAMIFY YOUR READ

Question 1

What are your customers' three favorite items of technology?

If you can answer this question, give yourself 1 point. If not, score 0.

This unprecedented engagement soon led players to start creating "locations within locations," sparking such good-natured competitions as battles over becoming the mayor of a coworker's private office. By changing the crux of the experience from focusing on purely random encounters with friends, the program designers created a structured engagement program that has since evolved to include challenges, prizes, status rewards, and collectible badges. Foursquare remains the undisputed mayor of the LBS world. By the spring of 2012, the company had achieved more than 2 billion check-ins. Averaging 3 million check-ins per day, Foursquare now offers support in 11 countries and a host of marketing options for enterprising partners.

Ultimately, Dodgeball and Foursquare's designers discovered that while they had clearly innovative ideas about checking in, all along *the game was the thing.* Without enough people investing in an underlying behavior alone (checking in), the value of the service was zero. However, by motivating people to play, the underlying behavior might follow. In the case of Foursquare, it did.

The Lesson from Foursquare's Experience

Foursquare's overall usage continues to grow, but many long-term users have become disenchanted with its services. This has led to some degree of hand-wringing about how well engagement mechanics like badges and challenges work over a longer period of time. One of the critical lessons in gamification from Foursquare is that there is a need for continuous improvement and innovation. Since its launch, Foursquare has released less than a handful of major updates to the product, including only a couple of revisions to the game play itself. In multiple discussions, the investors and founders have expressed a desire to move the company beyond its gaming roots to something more utilitarian—conducting functions like making restaurant recommendations and so on. But while this focus on alternate interactions may make sense for monetization, it appears to have had a negative effect on user engagement.

The key lesson: gamification is a process, not a product—and it requires long-term care and feeding. If you have a great gamified experience that consumers love and are using, don't turn away from it. *Lean into it*. That's the best way to ensure usage, revenue, and engagement in the long term. As many of the examples in this book show, making great gamified experiences can not only change your company's fortunes but they can even become a revenue stream in and of themselves.

Getting People to Pay Attention

The Foursquare example was not only remarkable for the mass engagement it ultimately engendered but even more so for the context in which it took place. When Dodgeball first launched in 2005, smartphone ownership in North America was at only 6 million. After that, the number of smartphone owners spiked: Morgan Stanley research has shown that, by the time Foursquare was revealed

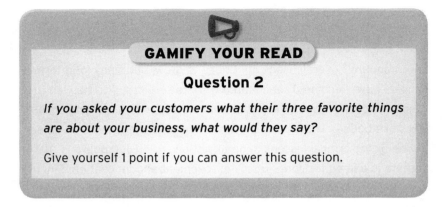

GAMIFY YOUR READ

Question 2

If you asked your customers what their three favorite things are about your business, what would they say?

Give yourself 1 point if you can answer this question.

(and Dodgeball killed) in 2009, handset makers had shipped over 51 million units. And only two short years later, smartphone shipments were outpacing PC sales, and the majority of phones in use were tipping in favor of iPhones and Androids—leaving former heavyweights RIM and Nokia struggling for oxygen.

Even major media channels are not immune. According to research from Nielsen, around 86 percent of U.S. adults with smart devices use a second screen—a phone or tablet—while watching TV. Gone are the days of sitting passively, staring at the tube. Now it's a 24/7 instant feedback culture with cowatching, tweeting, and socializing taking place throughout the media cycle.

NBC/Universal's USA Network was one of the first to take notice. Among the leaders in the gamification of major broadcast media, the company pioneered a social loyalty and gamified rewards program for its *Psych* TV show as early as 2009, leveraging technology from gamification provider Bunchball to deliver minigames to fans (Figure 8.2). From a trigger indicated by a graphic that ran in the lower third of the broadcast, users were prompted with questions and web-based "calls to action" that pushed them to the *Club Psych* website.

Once on the website, users were brought into games, prompted to complete challenges, and led into interactions with celebrities and other fans. Users could earn points that could be redeemed for merchandise and experiences, alongside an online store that

FIGURE 8.2 NBC/Universal's USA Network gamified the TV show *Psych* to create engagement with the fans.

sold *Psych* and NBC logo items for cash. Within weeks of the launch, online activity around the show increased over 100 percent, with key engagement metrics to match. Sales grew more than 50 percent at the online store as well, and the show's incremental web ad inventory was then used to drive further advertising revenue.

The dynamism of the *Psych* campaign demonstrates a sophisticated way to deliver surprise and delight with modalities that include badges for behavior, scratch-and-win lever pulls (for randomness), and bonus content available only to club members. By leaving some room for unexpected pleasure, the system becomes exponentially more compelling. Of course, the underlying emotional connection is quite simple: fun sells.

Luckily, the "breakthrough" lessons of *Psych* and Foursquare can be repeated—and many organizations have consequently developed comprehensive strategies aimed at generating attention and initial engagement using gamification. The six keys are these:

➤ Incorporate surprise and delight.
➤ Gamify your brand.
➤ Make it fun.
➤ Attract friends of friends to your brand.
➤ Be social to the core.
➤ Have a story—and tell it.

Of course, it goes without saying that you must make great products and/or offer great services. Gamification does not obviate the need for excellent product design and service delivery. On the contrary, the extensive socializing and self-determination in gamification may make great design even more important throughout the life of the game. Each one of the gamification strategies described here and in the following chapters can be used together or separately to heighten customer engagement. And an artful balance of approaches can create an exponentially more powerful outcome.

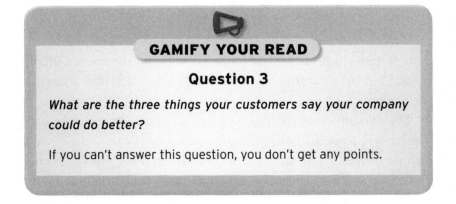

GAMIFY YOUR READ

Question 3

What are the three things your customers say your company could do better?

If you can't answer this question, you don't get any points.

Incorporate Surprise and Delight

While badges are common in most gamified apps and experiences, users don't know in advance all the badges they might earn on Foursquare. Typically, players get badges without forewarning when they cross a threshold that had been defined by the app's designers. Also, the paths to earning badges lack clear direction—in contrast to the well-marked paths that the Boy Scouts take to earn, for example, Woodcarving or Reading badges. In Foursquare, the players not being able to see it coming makes earning each badge an exciting "squee" moment, which raises the odds that engaged players will promote the game by announcing their accomplishments publicly on Facebook or Twitter.

This effect of surprise and delight leading to sharing has had a great deal of influence on the success of Foursquare—which isn't to say a quest-based approach like that of the Boy Scouts wouldn't have worked. But in the case of Foursquare, simply put, making it ridiculously easy, with minimal effort required, has really helped the company grow. With each shared check-in uploaded to users' social graphs—like Facebook walls and/or Twitter feeds—the contacts of those users were then exposed to the service, giving rise to its viral spread. Furthermore, as the amount of quantifiable data around each venue increased—largely driven by check-ins from badge-addicted users, Foursquare found itself positioned to explore the behaviors of more than just its users. The company could also pinpoint the locations they visited—and in some cases Foursquare could monetize those channels, using peer- and algorithm-driven recommendations underwritten by revenue from targeted ads and sponsorships.

Both the unprecedented shift in technology infrastructure and the early adoption by users enabled Foursquare growth and made it much more likely that the game mechanics the company implemented would succeed in engaging consumers. Without the iPhone, many functions (such as badges and simple check-ins) wouldn't have been possible, it's true. But in the era of the iPhone and the billions of downloaded games like *Angry Birds*, the market for user attention is more heated than ever. For Foursquare to break through in that environment, it couldn't just be novel or newsworthy. It wasn't enough that Foursquare founders Crowley and Selvadurai had lots of connected friends who were keen to stay in touch with their networks or even that the experience was fundamentally fun. It had to be all those things... and then some.

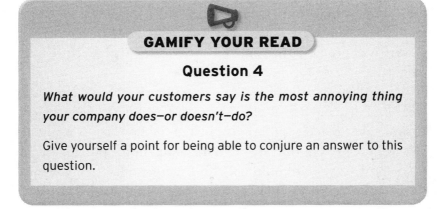

GAMIFY YOUR READ

Question 4

What would your customers say is the most annoying thing your company does—or doesn't—do?

Give yourself a point for being able to conjure an answer to this question.

Gamify Your Brand: The Nike+ Example

In 2004, Nike was already leading the way into the fledgling world of social networking by pairing with Gawker, an online media pioneer, to create a series of short films by up-and-coming filmmakers. At the time, Nike had already cinched the basketball shoe industry, but the company still lagged behind in other critical international sports arenas including soccer, baseball, and swimming. By 2006, Nike had fallen to its lowest market share ownership in the influential running shoe category, losing ground to Asics, New Balance, and other more "hard core" running shoe brands.

Then in 2006, something changed, and over the subsequent three years Nike became the undisputed leader in socially networked sports experiences. What changed in 2006 was that Nike developed a hardware and software solution featuring location-based technology that relied heavily on games called Nike+. Suddenly when individuals went for a run, they could track the number of steps they took, the calories they burned, and the routes they ran. Then, when they downloaded that information to their computer, their experience became even richer. Users could literally run races from Brooklyn with their best friends in Dallas, Los Angeles, or Hong Kong! They could encourage each other to beat fastest times, or they could find themselves compelled to go faster or further or harder in response to challenges, accolades, and prizes.

Thanks to Nike+, the company's share of the running market jumped nearly 10 percent in a single year. Building on this success, the Beaverton, Oregon–based apparel and footwear giant continued to innovate, adding even more gamified experiences designed to make running social, collaborative, and fun. What's more, as Nike's gamified strategies have taken root, the company has practically foregone traditional marketing altogether for a steady focus on digital distribution methods. And the reasons for that change are clear. Consider this: for a customer in the middle of an endless race against her brother who has just taken the lead, when it's time to invest in a new pair of shoes, you can bet it will have a swoosh on it.

Features of Nike+ include a cheering section made up of a user's Facebook friends and the ability for that user to challenge those same friends to a race. Nike+ also sends out electronic badges and prizes including videos of praise from celebrity athletes and other potential heroes. "Congratulations on completing your first 5K!" runner and two-time Olympic silver medalist Allyson Felix says in one Nike+ video reward—delivered "automagically" when that particular objective has been achieved.

Setting aside all the bells and whistles, Nike+ has leveraged a very simple concept—beating your personal best—to create a kind of rapid feedback gamification system. Driving people to greatness fits well with the Nike brand, and by mid-2012, Nike+ had over 5 million users who had run a collective 450 million miles. To put that into perspective, the Sporting Goods Manufacturers

Association (SGMA) has estimated that there are only 9 million frequent runners in America, averaging over 110 runs per year. But Nike's major market is composed of the 38 million Americans who casually run or jog at least once every two months—rather than just the hard-core. So while Nike+ had had a quick run to capturing nearly 50 percent of the hard-core market, after it developed the first Nike+ applications, the company needed something even more radical to capture the mass market.

GAMIFY YOUR READ

Question 5

What three business or cultural icons do your customers most look up to?

Give yourself a point, as always, if you can answer this question.

So in 2012, Nike launched the *FuelBand*—one of the most successful products in the company's history. The FuelBand, which measures movement and connects to Nike+ to monitor user training experience within the game, sold out instantly when preorders became available. Through celebrity promotion, spectacular viral promotion, and product versioning, the FuelBand may perhaps have become the hardest-to-get hardware device since iPhones and iPads were launched to massive shortages. Recently, tying the whole concept together, Nike has launched *GameOnWorld,* which is a direct acknowledgment and homage to their gamified core strategy.

This marketing campaign from Nike puts its core customers—fitness buffs—into a video game layered over the real world. The customers compete to beat their personal best, complete challenges, and beat characters like famous tough-guy actor Ving Rhames to level up. In essence, the company has made gamification core to its product design and global marketing strategy.

On a deeper level, the reason why Nike+ and the FuelBand have been so successful is that they have delivered on the promise of the game itself: to help you achieve and beat your personal best. Clearly this has been the basic message of the advertising for companies like Nike for decades. But connecting the dots between actual marketing achievement and a pair of running shoes is an obvious challenge dependent on a level of customer attention to detail that just doesn't happen in the untethered world. Through their feedback-based gamification approach, Nike follows its customers every step of the way. When they succeed, Nike (and its products) is right there—giving them the good news, cheering them on, reminding them to push themselves. It's the kind of dialogue that most brands dream of but only gamification can deliver.

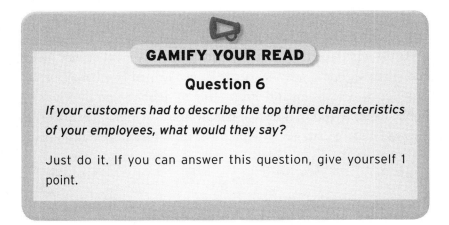

GAMIFY YOUR READ

Question 6

If your customers had to describe the top three characteristics of your employees, what would they say?

Just do it. If you can answer this question, give yourself 1 point.

Make It Fun

Delivering fun and exhilaration was something that Apple's Steve Jobs profoundly understood in his life. A consummate showman, his Apple product unveiling speeches were legendary. Each time, the audience waited with baited breath for him to say the magic words… "And one more thing."

But in the run-up to each hot-ticket launch event, Apple PR began to use subtle gamification to signal (or toy with) the media in attendance. Although the company was famously tight-lipped about product launches—leaks were causes for immediate dismissal from the company—the PR team began a habit of stealthily building in clues to the event *around* its launch, including within the invitation to the launch itself.

Speculation on the Internet was always at a fever pitch before the events, but the PR team's choices were especially interesting. For example, in the invitation to the iPhone 4S reveal, there were several interesting clues as to what new features the product had to offer. Using the word "talk" in the opening clue pointed to the launch of Siri voice recognition. By making the choice to use the singular iPhone—instead of the plural iPhones—the company was insinuating that the upcoming announcement wasn't about *all* incarnations of the iPhone but rather of one in particular. Also, placing a number 4 in the calendar established both the operating system as well as the date of the launch.

Users who received the invitation or who were otherwise lucky enough to see one in advance of the launch helped build buzz for the product by discussing and attempting to disseminate the clues in public forums. Today, now that people know to look, they are looking hard. Before a launch on September 12, 2012, a simple announce-

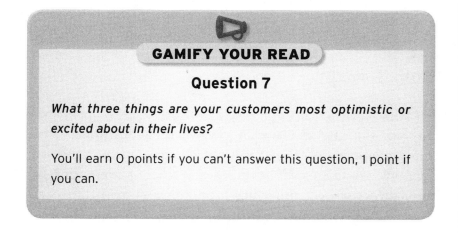

GAMIFY YOUR READ

Question 7

What three things are your customers most optimistic or excited about in their lives?

You'll earn 0 points if you can't answer this question, 1 point if you can.

ment went out featuring the words "It's almost here" above a large black number 12 with a shadowy image of the number 5 below it. Speculation grew like wildfire around the Internet with people arguing points such as the idea that Apple wasn't going to continue naming iPhones by number, so the 5 had to indicate five products being launched at once. (It turned out that the invitation was for the iPhone 5, perhaps to the disappointment of some clever decoders.)

The results of Apple's little invitation game have been astonishing—even by the company's standards. According to Google, there have been over 4 million blog posts and web mentions devoted **solely** to the topic of decoding these invitations. While this is a small drop in the bucket of the total earned media related to Apple launches, it nonetheless represents substantial free promotion—and likely hundreds of millions of dollars in incremental revenue for the company. Clearly, designers and executives have enjoyed—and profited immensely from—this little bit of fun.

But fun sells and not just in consumer electronics. It works for even more august brands and experiences, and even in places you might not expect. The luxury women's shoemaker Jimmy Choo decided to play a game with its customers for the rollout of a new line of tennis shoes in 2010. Bucking the convention that women—especially those interested in high-end footwear—might be adverse to a little healthy competition, Jimmy Choo used the streets of London as its game board and social networks as its platform in a game called *CatchAChoo*.

Players were given the opportunity to win one of six pairs of trainers if they were quick to discover their "hidden," but real location in London. The company announced these locations via Facebook, Twitter, and Foursquare. The first player to find the Jimmy Choo staffer stationed casually at the location and announce, "I've been following you!" won. An unprecedented 20,000 people played the game that sunny day, making it the single biggest promotional event for the company in its history. Additionally, hundreds of thousands more women followed along remotely (only Londoners could play), driven by tremendous buzz and social media support.

It's believed that Jimmy Choo spent well under $100,000 to run this promotion, while driving millions in earned media and the adoration and enthusiasm of female fans worldwide.

Other famous brands have used fun to get the world's attention in close synergy with their brand. MINI Cooper asked consumers in Stockholm to "hunt and catch" their new Countryman model in 2010. When players got within 50 meters of the car, they could "take it" virtually by clicking an app on their smartphones. They were then alerted to nearby "enemies" that were labeled as such on the map feature within the app. The goal was for the player in possession of the car to stay at least 50 meters away from other players. The first person who successfully kept the car for a week won the actual car.

In a similar vein, the German telecommunications giant Deutsche Telekom ran a live-action version of the popular mobile game *Angry Birds* in the center of Barcelona during the 3GSM conference. Using a tablet, users pulled back on the familiar rubber band to launch a bird into the air. Once released, however, a "real live" angry bird went flying into a physical wood and pigs structure. Although only a few dozen people got to play the game live, there were thousands watching it take place live in Barcelona that day, and over 15 million have since watched the video on YouTube. The display is now being hailed by such websites as ForeverGeek as one of the greatest ad campaigns ever executed.

Watch video of the amazing live action *Angry Birds* game, and get easy access to many other examples highlighted in this chapter by accessing *The Gamification Revolution* app at http://gamrev.com.

Using a more loyalty-oriented approach, Tabasco recently launched an ambassador program called *Tabasco Nation*. The gamified engagement campaign uses Facebook as a platform to mobilize its fan base of 500,000 people. Based around challenges, users are asked to count up the number of drops of Tabasco sauce they consume daily, upload photos of interesting food combinations, and take a series of daily polls. Players are awarded with points, badges, Tabasco brand–related prizes, and titles like Ambassador

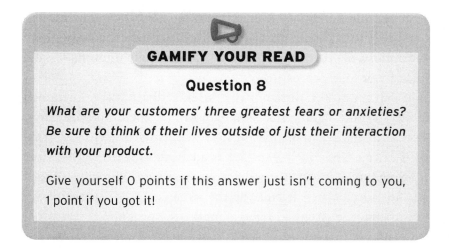

GAMIFY YOUR READ

Question 8

What are your customers' three greatest fears or anxieties? Be sure to think of their lives outside of just their interaction with your product.

Give yourself 0 points if this answer just isn't coming to you, 1 point if you got it!

and Mayor. But the game is expanding. In one challenge the company is calling the *Tabasco National Anthem*, users will engage in a "never-ending video" of people handing off a bottle of Tabasco sauce from person to person.

These are models that work and work well. Those that integrate socializing directly into the users' experience are especially noteworthy. Rather than being an afterthought, social networking is core to the experience—that is, you can't progress without it.

Attract Friends of Friends to Your Brand

Obviously, fun—even in a smaller, bite-sized form—is a powerful tool for generating interest and engagement among users. However, many gamelike designs simply aren't up to the task of spreading the word. While this is especially true of winner-take-all contests (in which you have an express disincentive to invite anyone else to play) and simple refer-a-friend forms (that drive spammy or low-value behavior), the use of social networking in most consumer promotions is laughable.

An Element Bar is a custom-made "whole food bar," which consumers can design online. The Element Bar is like a granola bar, but the granola itself is optional. Users of the Element Bar company's website can log in and design their own box of 12 bars, choosing from the ingredients described and offered by the company. The bars are touted as being "all natural" and healthier than other market options because they are made without high amounts of saturated fat or food processing.

From the outset, the company's user feedback was tremendous. It was so good, in fact, that Jonathan Miller, one of the company's two founders, began wondering how to leverage the segment of the consumer base actively working as advocates for the brand. Considering the LivingSocial model whereby people who sell a specific deal to three of their friends get the same deal for free, he decided to implement a gamified referral marketing program.

Critically, Miller understood that his program would have to accomplish more than just creating "buzz" or "social media mentions." He cared a great deal about tying gamification to sales metrics, and he wanted to ensure that he could track every action users took on the company's website. To begin, he analyzed the ways users communicated on social networks, paying close attention to how they recommended products to friends or followers. He devised a simple metric that would be both trackable and easy for users to follow: "In the early version it was 'tell a friend, send an e-mail,'" he explained. Thus, if customers brought in other customers, everyone was rewarded. "You either got a discount, or you got the product for free."

However, Miller knew that not everyone was keen on publicly praising products. He cites two main inhibitors to nailing a positive referral: (1) People who have never tried a particular product, at a behavioral level, are less likely than people who have used it to offer praise, even if that praise is incentivized. (2) People don't like being blasted with something like an advertisement even if it comes from a friend, and they are therefore hesitant to blast anyone themselves.

For the Element Bars, Miller decided that the best way to strategize was to pull instead of push—so the company created a game. Because sites like Facebook and Twitter don't actually show everything everyone posts in everyone's feeds every time, Element Bars figured out that the company had to generate a lot of traffic in a short amount of time to get the most visibility. It was this visibility alone that made the game financially viable, especially considering that the company had a product that could be turned into a prize.

The very first thing the company did was offer a free case of bars to the winner of a sweepstakes. To enter, all you had to do was like the Element Bars Facebook page. Within the first hour that the program started, the page achieved eight times more likes than ever before. By the end of day one, the page had more than 5,000 likes. On day two, players could enter a new sweepstakes by adding a comment to the news feed or naming their favorite ingredient to put in an Element Bar. Immediately comments began adding up as users spread the love.

The game has tracked how many people have been exposed to the company's brand, how many people have engaged with it, and how many people, as a result of a friend's engagement, have started interacting with the company anew. Element Bars has seen its number of monthly likes increase threefold. It has also reported a huge increase in activity with its brand page. More importantly in terms of the goals of the small company, its reach grew to three times the normal amount, meaning that user engagement led to contact with their customers' friends, and their customers' friends of friends, and so on.

Be Social to the Core

Most successful social games—especially those on Facebook—understand the optimal social promotion dynamic exceedingly well. If your social request or promotion is a secondary action in a gamified experience (for example, if you use a refer-a-friend form), you will get out exactly what users put in—low-quality, low-priority, low-intention action. In summary, spam.

But there is another way. Pioneered by games like *Cafe World,* a restaurant-owning game on Facebook, new models have emerged that put social requests directly in the line of game play. In other words, getting people to play the game *is part of the game.* For example, when players need to progress to the next level in *Cafe World*, they are prompted to recruit friends to play. If their friends accept, the players receive virtual currency or other items that are necessary to progress. When their invitation is dispatched, their friends receive a notice that there is something for them (for example, an extra cake to offer) or that something is needed of them (for example, the player needs some eggs), and they are invited to partake or assist.

Progression, which is a key element in an overall sense of happiness and mastery, is gated by this social interaction. The recipient of the request—typically a friend—is clued into the fact that the achievement of the player is gated by their action or inaction. Thus, social pressure successfully leads to recruiting other players, which translates into incrementally increasing numbers of users and revenue for the experience.

In 2011, Intuit made waves for its highly successful gamified social campaign. The company's TurboTax brand leveraged the power of social networking and philanthropy by launching its *Gaming for Good*. This Facebook-based memory card game was simple: remember like items that qualify for tax deductibility on screen, and then match them all to complete up to three levels of play. For each game completed, TurboTax made a donation to the Toys for Tots charity.

The program blew the doors off of all previous stats for user acquisition. TurboTax gained over 101,000 new Facebook fans in just a few short weeks, with each fan averaging over 1.44 "stream" messages (posts to Facebook or Twitter), spending nearly eight minutes per session playing the game. On top of that, the daily average number of people talking about TurboTax rose precipitously, going from 300 people per day to over 43,000 at its peak. Their viral reach—a measurement of the number of people who saw TurboTax messages—also rose from just around 2,500 to over 300,000 people per day.

The fact that the app promised a charitable donation proved a big part of its success, demonstrating that users will make an extra effort to support charitable causes with their time. Designed by Vitrue, the TurboTax game also cleverly showed the total number of toys being donated by the company by displaying a counter. Therefore, players could see the direct effect of their action on the charity as they played—and could collaboratively engage to improve the outcome. The game itself was overly simplistic, and it would not have been able to sustain engagement in the long term, but as a powerful short-term social vehicle, it was perfect for TurboTax.

Although TurboTax's approach to social gamification was successful for the brand, one element that wasn't core to the experience was a story. Not every gamified experience has to focus strongly on story, but when the brand lends itself well to narrative, amazing consumer interactions are possible.

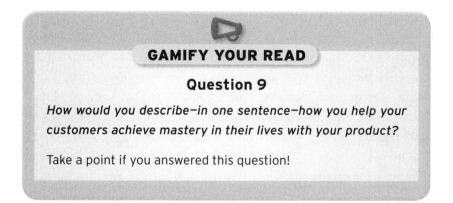

GAMIFY YOUR READ

Question 9

How would you describe—in one sentence—how you help your customers achieve mastery in their lives with your product?

Take a point if you answered this question!

Have a Story—and Tell It

One summer in 2007, a well-told story was exactly what the people of San Diego helped to tell. At the San Diego Comic-Con, more than 10,000 real-world players took to the streets in a viral marketing campaign anticipating the release of the film *The Dark Knight*. Over the course of play, the game rallied in excess of 3 million players worldwide. But more than that, it built a community that called itself the Joker's Army. These players dynamically responded to the orders of their leader, completing challenges, including donning Joker-like face paint and photographing themselves in front of landmarks worldwide.

Helmed by former Disney imagineer and game design veteran Susan Bonds, 42 Entertainment masterminded the campaign. The company's projects are remarkable not only because of their scale but also because of the ways in which they utilize technology across the board, creating user experiences that leverage every major device—while bleeding a fictional narrative into "real life."

Why So Serious?, the name of the *Dark Knight* game, was based on a memorable line uttered by Heath Ledger's Joker in the film. The game kicked off when joker cards were dropped in strategic locations such as comic book stores and events where a core audience might be found. The cards directed players to a website where they had to enter their e-mail address to vote in a virtual Gotham City election. The vote was for or against Harvey Dent, a character who would be central to the film. Almost immediately 20,000 players signed up. Those 20,000 were encouraged to bring in other players when they were shown part of a secret photograph. As the photo slowly revealed itself, it became known that 100,000 players were required to completely uncover the image. The media became interested. Buzz was building. When the game hit 100,000 players, the image appeared: it was the face of the Joker. But it didn't last. The image subsequently faded to a black screen, and an ominous message underscored by laughter read: "See you in December."

Susan Bonds, in a keynote address at the New York GSummit in 2011, explained that the purpose of fading out the image was simple. Players who had seen it felt special, as if they were part of an exclusive club. For everyone else who only heard about the image, there was something legendary about it having appeared at all. But most of all, that image changed the conversation, it increased engagement, and it left players wondering, "What's next?"

The San Diego scavenger hunt intentionally coincided with Comic-Con. Using 10,000 marked dollar bills, players were given a location from which to begin. Once there, an airplane flew overhead writing a phone number in the sky. Players called the number to find out their next instruction, which included painting themselves in the likeness of the Joker. Face paints were handed out and players complied. At the end of the hunt, one lucky player was selected out of the crowd to be taken to the film set where he actually got to play one of the Joker's henchmen in the film!

The game continued over the next months until the film's release. Challenges were issued around the country. Some players saw a notice to visit certain bakeries in various cities. There they had to offer up a code phrase in order to receive a clue. The game was first come, first served, but those who made it to the bakeries in time were given a cake bearing a number and the words "Call me now." Suddenly the cake in front of them began to ring. When the players dug through the icing and cake, they discovered an evidence bag inside of which was a ringing cell phone. From that point forward they were advised that they would ultimately be part of the efforts to spring the Joker from jail, a pivotal point in the movie itself.

Why So Serious? was an overwhelming success in the world of viral marketing. By finding, engaging, and then re-engaging not just an audience but a *community of people*, fans of the *Batman* franchise went from passive observers to active participants. Whereas 10 years ago people who liked *Batman* bought the toys and went to the movies, *Why So Serious?* made it clear that, based on the rabid fan interest it had inspired, the stakes are higher today, in large part due to the gamification of the advertising of the films.

The game itself was loud and very public. Even people who weren't playing probably overheard something about it going on— either on the web, on the news, or via social media. In 1939, when the world was introduced to a winged superhero fighting the criminal element on the nighttime streets of Gotham City, a simple black-and-white ad in the back of a comic book was enough to garner attention. Batman, with his cool toys and his skills with his bat weapons, was all that was needed. But today we are inundated with so much information, so many things to do with our free time, and so little free time to begin with, where do we look? Or even more important, how do you get us to look?

For years people have argued which superhero would win in direct hero-to-hero combat. When it comes to branding and advertising, Batman wins. And with it, so does gamification. As the most powerful tool for cutting through the noise and connecting with audiences, gamification can be used with a wide range of design approaches and strategies. Critically, you must have a great product and story to tell about it. Place an emphasis on fun that leverages surprise and delight appropriately, while ensuring integral sociability at every turn, and you can help kick-start your customer engagement process. Once that's under way, your focus can—and should—turn to building lasting engagement.

GAMIFY YOUR READ

Point Game: Follow Your Dreams!

Count up your points. If you have 5 points or more, your business is primed and ready to **snag the customers of your dreams.**

Head over to *The Gamification Revolution* app at http://gam rev.com and share your experiences with your colleagues and friends. You can also keep score, unlock bonus content, share the book with others, and access key online resources in a single step.

9

SUSTAINING
LONG-TERM CUSTOMER
ENGAGEMENT

★

No matter how good the design of your initial customer engagement process, at some point users of your system will lose interest, and their interaction with it will begin to atrophy. Even the best designed and most expensive games in history are not immune to the pitfalls of user fatigue or distraction from newer, more exciting games.

Take, for example, *Star Wars Old Republic*. The massively multiplayer online (MMO) game, developed at a cost of between $150 and $200 million, is considered the most expensive game experience ever developed. Built over a number of years by the critically lauded team at BioWare, the game's hotly anticipated launch was nothing short of spectacular. After years of intense consumer scrutiny and interest, the game debuted in December 2011 and amassed over 1 million subscribers within three days. The game was an instant hit, delivering more context for character development than any previous game of its ilk. Players received their own starships and access to multiple planets along with the possibility for deep narrative expansion, especially if players teamed up.

The early spike in player onboarding made it the biggest launch and fastest growing MMOG in history. But after peaking at nearly 2

GAMIFY YOUR READ

Solve the Sentence Anagram

Collect all the words in boldface type scattered throughout this chapter (chapter headings don't count). Then rearrange those words to answer this question:

What industry's gamified programs repeatedly yield the least fun and offer no value and meager rewards—yet are ripe with fresh opportunities for all three?

For the answer, visit *The Gamification Revolution* app, which can be downloaded at http://gamrev.com, or verify the answer in the answer key at the back of the book.

million subscribers, a scant 60 days later, traffic began to fall. Within eight months usage dropped below the game's opening 1 million number, impacting Electronic Arts' financial situation significantly enough to warrant a special discussion on their quarterly earnings call. The company, in a desperate attempt to generate greater interest in the game, announced it would switch from the subscription of $13 per month to a free-to-play model (where revenue comes from the sale of virtual items) by the fourth quarter of 2012.

Similar, though less dramatic fates have befallen many other online game experiences, including the much-vaunted *World of Warcraft*—one of the longest running **and** most successful MMOGs of all time, which lost 1 million subscribers in a single month in 2012. Other companies like Zynga and Rovio—publishers that deal in hundreds of millions, or billions, of players—have seen their fortunes swing by huge variants as well.

The question on every product or marketing executive's mind immediately is, of course, "Why?" Unsurprisingly, game industry execs wonder the same thing. There are no easy answers, and many different factors play into the equation including changing tastes, perceived value for money, and social congregation around particular games. Ultimately, however, they all resolve to a single, critical point: *the game just isn't fun enough anymore.* Once users lose interest or motivation, it's exceedingly hard to get them back. And once their friends leave, en masse, it's even harder to keep them around and to find new players.

So if even games companies—with their substantial resources and behavioral knowledge—are not immune to player fatigue, what hope do other industries and brands have for sustaining engagement?

While the answer will be different for every company and vertical, there are some strategies that successful organizations have used to build lasting engagement through gamification:

- ➤ Define a grind.
- ➤ Build a powerful engagement loop.
- ➤ Keep content fresh.
- ➤ Use meaningful incentives.
- ➤ Make it personal, and design it for mastery.
- ➤ Create continuous learning opportunities.
- ➤ Monetize loyalty.

Let's take a closer look at these approaches and how they are being used by successful organizations.

Define a Grind

In game terms, a *grind* is a simple activity that users must regularly repeat in order to earn enough resources to progress in the game. Typically, the grind is a simple activity (or set of activities) that can be accomplished fairly mindlessly over and over again. Doing it yields a unit of currency that—when done enough—can be used to advance more substantially in a game. Typically, this grind might be something like harvesting a plant or mining a metal as seen in many role-playing games. In the workaday world, something like punching your time clock, answering customer support calls, or holding your weekly standing meeting might qualify as grinds.

In gamified systems, the grind is typically a small unit of action that closely corresponds to a basic behavior that users must complete in order to progress. For example, in Foursquare, the grind is checking into locations. In Instagram—the ultrapopular photosharing social network—the grind is uploading a picture. For supermarket stock people, stocking shelves is the grind. For mail carriers, visiting mailboxes is the grind. Of course, all of these things are made up of more than one action. In Foursquare the user must get out the mobile device, click several buttons, and finally check in. **Supermarkets** enlist employees to unpack boxes, locate like items, and stock shelves. Mail carriers must go to a depot, get a huge pile of items to deliver, sort them, and then deliver them from mailbox to mailbox. However, as most of us know from other grinds in our lives (like brushing teeth), the series of actions becomes fairly automatic over time.

And therein lies its power. Once you become accustomed to doing the behavior, it becomes second nature. As a habit-forming minibehavior, a grind forms the foundation of most gamified systems. The trick is to identify, highlight, and drive grinding behavior in gamified experiences to maximize usage as well as the outcome of that usage.

Once users are accustomed to a grind and they have been trained to do the grind based on a trigger (arriving at a location, taking a picture, getting behind the wheel of a car, and some other action), you can build more complex behaviors on top of it.

Build an Engagement Loop

Behind every successful consumer app, there is a thoughtful, well-designed engagement loop. Although it may seem trivial, the design and execution of this core element can determine success or failure for your organization's engagement strategy. But what exactly is an engagement loop, and why does it matter so much?

As we've established throughout this book, consumers are increasingly distracted. If you **don't** make a deliberate effort to engage them on a regular basis, odds are they will lose interest in your product or service. Specifically, you need to consider what drives their behavior, design a hook that brings them into your product, and then allow them to express a social action, which you respond to with a trigger to bring them back. You can imagine this interaction in the form of a virtuous cycle (Figure 9.1).

The cycle is composed of four elements: a motivating emotion, a social call to action, user re-engagement, and visible progress and **rewards**. To better understand how they work, let's look closely at Instagram, a highly successful, viral product. The company, which

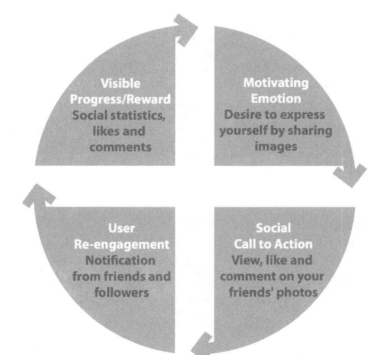

FIGURE 9.1 For the photosharing social network Instagram, the viral loop driving user engagement and new user acquisition might look like this.

was founded by Mike Krieger and Kevin Systrom in 2010, raised a total of $57 million in venture capital and was sold to Facebook for $1 billion in April 2012. The site allows users to easily take a photo, modify it with a series of filters, and then share it **with** other Instagram users as well as friends on social networks like Facebook and Twitter. The company's astronomical selling price was based largely on its viral success: starting with 100,000 early adopters in October 2010, it had more than 80 million active users by mid-July 2012—an addition of nearly 10 million new users per month. These stats are impressive by any measure. How did they do it?

The gamified, viral loop inherent in Instagram goes a long way toward explaining its success.

Motivating emotion. Instagram allows users to act on the desire to express themselves and to share the cool things they see. It lets them demonstrate that they have a keen eye, a sense of humor or aesthetic beauty, and a creative flair (which they can show off by way of available photo filters).

Social call to action. The system is designed to let users easily scroll through a friend's photos, liking them and/or commenting on them.

User re-engagement. When others like or comment on a user's photos, they receive a notification that brings them back to the app.

Visible progress and rewards. Users can see the total likes and comments on each photo, plus their aggregate stats.

What's notable about the design of Instagram's viral loop is how tight it is. Certainly, the app would not have had the same level of success were it not for an appealing user experience. However, because the engagement process was well integrated into the experience, users were brought back to the app in a continuous cycle of content consumption and creation that activated their intrinsic desire to engage with others. This facilitates both customer acqui-

Melissa Chow's Like-A-Hug

Designed as a part of Hiroshi Ishii's tangible interfaces course at the MIT Media Lab, this vest actually inflates every time someone likes your status on Facebook. The vest's "hug" symbolizes the feeling of warmth that social networking users get from the engagement loop provided by likes and comments, turning them from the virtual to the literal. While the product is intentionally pushing boundaries and unlikely to become a serious fashion trend any time soon, the metaphor is unmistakable: a like is like a hug without having to squeeze.

Download *The Gamification Revolution* app at http://gamrev.com to watch Melissa Chow's Like-A-Hug in action! You can also check out all the other engagement programs we discuss in more detail while you analyze your favorites.

sition and retention and really helps drive their content creation engine—a key element in a successful gamification strategy.

Keep Content Fresh

One detail that doesn't escape Dan Porter, chief executive officer of OMGPOP, is how important it is to consistently churn out hits when you're selling to consumers. The company, which started in 2006 as iminlikewithyou.com, was one of the pioneers of gamified interactions. OMGPOP built a game-based dating and flirting site that eventually morphed into a games site targeting a youthful demographic. Despite its thriving community and a wide assortment of games, it wasn't until it launched *Draw Something*—the runaway iPhone hit game—that Zynga came calling. In early 2012, the company was acquired by Zynga for $180 million.

Draw Something allows you to play a game resembling *Pictionary* on mobile devices (Figure 9.2). Working together with a friend, you draw an image that represents a phrase **or** concept. Your partner then has to guess what your drawing means. The app skyrocketed to the top of the world game charts shortly after its release,

FIGURE 9.2 *Draw Something*–the collaborative and social blockbuster game–asks one player to draw a clue and the other to guess what's in the picture.

becoming an international sensation. It was the coup de grace for the company, which had spent the better part of five years churning through socially networked flash minigames—or short video games, often a game within a larger video game—on its site.

The company needed to **offer** an array of different, ever-changing games to drive and sustain user interest. As one became old, losing traction among users, it would be replaced by a new one. As with many game sites that deliver a catalog of various game choices, OMGPOP needed to balance the consumer need for fresh content with the cost of producing it. Unlike TV, where syndication offers content a long tail of monetization that can sometimes run for years, casual games rarely get this option. This naturally constrains the budgets for these games, hampering a company's ability to make money.

In order to keep the content fresh in a cost-effective way, it became critical to find a way for users to generate interesting experiences for each other. So OMGPOP looked for games that people would want to play over and over again, and *Draw Something* seemed ideal. The principal ongoing expense of the game was to create new clues for users to draw, which was a fairly cheap and easy prospect. The same clue could even be replayed with different friends since players draw differently. It was this particular endless and expansive interaction that rocketed the company to fame and fortune.

Shortly after the Zynga acquisition, *Draw Something* saw the same fate as the MMOGs *Star Wars Old Republic* and *World of Warcraft* mentioned earlier. After doing a great job of generating initial buzz and engagement, usage began to drop off. Though *Draw Something* had delivered many dynamic innovations, there was still what might be called a *freshness gap*—that is, the company failed to deliver new kinds of interactions. Though the pictures and clues evolved, the core game play stayed the same. Soon, the tightly bound social networks that had propelled the game forward in the first place began to fray—and as your friends stop playing, so do you.

The key element to remember is that for users to return every hour or day or week or month, new, surprising, and interesting activities and interactions must be regularly available. Fresh content alone isn't enough. Consider how most engagement systems—like loyalty **programs**—deal with introducing new mechanics.

In the decades leading up to the 2010s, most **loyalty** programs made small program tweaks—on average—only once every few years. In the past decade, that pace of change has begun to increase rapidly. From 2011 to 2012 alone, as many as a third of major travel loyalty programs in the United States made significant changes to their programs. These included new top-tier status levels (Starwood) and ways to earn points, as well as special recognition for ultra-long-term fliers (United Airlines). United Airlines, for example, now officially recognizes 2- and 3-million-mile fliers with codified benefits that were previously kept secret—a reflection of the program's longevity.

Historically, many of these changes were made to improve the operating economics of the programs themselves. Companies avoided making the changes for fear of alienating their best customers and creating market tension and confusion. Today, the act of making changes has become as important as the changes themselves. Tweaks surely give users and the press something to talk about. But they also create new and exciting **challenges** for players to engage with, keeping the game fresh well beyond its sell-by date. Tied to most of these structural changes, of course, are shifts in incentives designed to drive specific behavior.

Use Meaningful Incentives

By maintaining or creating incentives and rewards that are meaningful, players are more likely to play and keep playing. Nowhere is this truer than when dealing with long-term customer engagement and retention. A prime example has been the recent transformation of the waste management industry by some highly successful, long-term incentive designs.

RecycleBank, founded in 2004, has raised over $80 million to prove a simple idea: if consumers are given a gamified incentive to recycle, their rate of recycling will increase. Since that time, the company has helped over 300 communities and 3 million households divert hundreds of millions of pounds of recyclables away from landfills.

The consumer experience is simple: sign up and receive a recycling bin with a special radio frequency identification (RFID) tag. The bin is weighed at every collection and, based on the volume of recycling, a certain number of "recycling bucks" are deposited in the customer's account. This virtual currency can then be redeemed for merchandise, discounts, or charitable contributions through the company's thousands of merchandising partners, which are also, cleverly, the sources of funding for the incentives (Figure 9.3).

What RecycleBank has learned is that ongoing engagement requires the right incentives—both tangible and emotional. The

FIGURE 9.3 RecycleBank gives consumers points and rewards for recycling using innovative RFID technologies and brand partnerships.

company takes great care to ensure that its partners are closely aligned with RecycleBank's target demographic: mothers in their early forties and younger. By maintaining a continuous stream of new redemption options, the system remains interesting and helps to ensure that the main behavior (recycling) continues to be a user priority.

Beyond discounts and free merchandise, RecycleBank's research discovered that its consumers were seeking an opportunity to connect with others as well as challenge themselves. The company has used this knowledge to ensure that rewards are aligned with those interests, delivering experiences that allow moms to connect with their kids through RecycleBank and also to challenge themselves (and their neighbors) to contests—all for bragging rights. For example, RecycleBank ran a *Green Your Home* game that challenged families to reduce their ecofootprints and submit photos to prove it. Those photos were shared socially and judged against others from the community. Prizes including a valuable home makeover helped drive participation, but it was the satisfaction of becoming "greener" than your neighbor that kept people playing.

Both physical and virtual rewards need to activate an emotional need for gratification in addition to—and sometimes instead of—the need for cash-value prizes.

Make It Personal and Design It for Mastery

The most important element of RecycleBank's success is how well it ties into the individual's desire for mastery and a sense of progress—in other words, the company provides achievable goals with opportunities for meaningful advancement. For people who care about the environment, RecycleBank offers that critical sense of agency—or the sense that you have control over your destiny. It helps foster this through instant feedback in the form of statistics indicating how much one small behavioral change can impact the world. For example, the company shares with its users just how many tons of recycling you, your community, and others in the

RecycleBank community at large have diverted from landfills. The company does what day-to-day environmentally conscious actions cannot otherwise do: *deliver tangible evidence of progress*. No doubt this contributes handily to the 90 percent recycling rates the company has been able to achieve in some jurisdictions.

That sense of progress and mastery is considered by many theorists to be central to what makes gamified experiences—and indeed, life—fun. The conceit is that we all have a desire to achieve mastery over various areas of our life, and systems that allow us to do that will be perceived as fun or particularly meaningful. Additionally, the more the system can show us the progress we've made along the track to our goal, the more likely we are to stick to it.

Most gamified fitness systems, such as Nike+ (as discussed in detail in Chapter 8), understand this particularly well—and they **use** the concept of progression to mastery effectively to drive long-term engagement with customers by tracking their ongoing fitness accomplishments.

Another fitness solution that has had a particularly outsized effect is Zamzee, and its use of feedback and progression to mastery has been extraordinary.

The company, incubated in HopeLab in the San Francisco Bay Area, makes a small accelerometer that you clip to or wear on your clothes (Figure 9.4). As you move throughout the day, the Zamzee tracks your motion, giving you an estimated number of steps taken and distances traveled. This information is available on Zamzee's gamified fitness portal, which is accessible once you plug in your device to your computer at the end of the day. There, you can see your movement over time, earn points for your actions, and redeem them for virtual and physical prizes that matter to you. You can even socialize your actions with your friends and see how your community is doing.

The effect of Zamzee's focus on long-term engagement has paid off. The company has demonstrated that it's been able to get users to add the equivalent of one whole marathon to their monthly movement using the device and its accompanying service. Over the

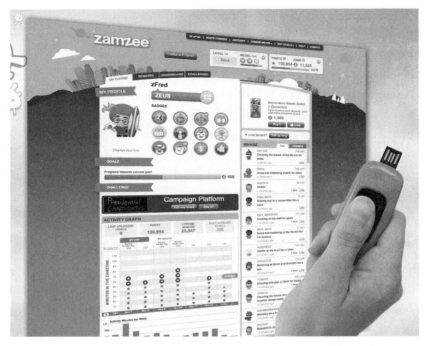

FIGURE 9.4 Zamzee's activity meter tracks kids' movements, letting them compete to see their fitness progress.

longer term, the company's research has indicated that Zamzee was able to drive an increase of 59 percent in physical activity among kids using the service. What makes the story even more exciting is that the targeted user population is children in lower socioeconomic environments—those who are statistically at the highest risk for diabetes and other health issues related to obesity and poor physical fitness.

Critically, as kids progress through Zamzee's system, they can see their progress—and that of their friends—shown over the arc of their usage. This allows them to really experience what they've accomplished every time, and the system continuously reminds them of the progress they've made through stats, badges, and other game mechanics.

To maintain a feeling that you're making progress—or heading toward mastery—is especially difficult to achieve in physical fitness. The problem is compounded by the fact that it typically takes weeks for your body to start showing positive signs of the effect of increased movement and reduced weight. Therefore, by providing immediate feedback in the form of "minutes moved" (Zamzee's principal metric), the system can offer positive feedback before Mother Nature can catch up. Similarly, for any strategy you may deploy to get customers engaged over a hump or plateau, it's especially important that you leverage each of the engagement patterns described here. Balancing them the way Zamzee does will yield the improved engagement you seek.

Create Continuous Learning Opportunities

A more specific aspect of the drive toward mastery is user-driven learning. As the options for online education and knowledge proliferate, customers are increasingly interested in learning as an activity separate from pure utility. For example, they want to *both* be able to bank online easily *and* increase their financial literacy. Similarly, there has been a marked rise in the demand for language education (and multilingualism), driven by the growth of globalization as well as migration. As more and more customers engage with new technologies, they'll want—and need—to learn myriad new skills.

These new online education customers aren't the same as those of yore for whom reading the entire 30-page manual before picking up the new camera was par for the course. Too impatient to even watch a three-minute training video before using a product, the new customers want to *try out* an offer right away. At the same time, they want to be taught the underlying concepts, technologies, and ideas so that they can make progress toward their life goals. And along the way, they expect positive reinforcement. If your business has a pedagogical bent, this becomes even more important.

So how do you speak to these new customers who demand education at every turn? You deliver a gamified learning system that creates, sustains, and rewards engagement, like Codecademy.

This hot NYC-based start-up is on a mission to help people learn how to write software.

The site, which is backed by some of the biggest venture capitalists in the United States, taught over 1 million people to code in under a year—making it one of the biggest science, technology, engineering, and math (STEM) teaching programs in history. Codecademy uses the principles of gamification to drive learning, including awarding badges, points, and levels.

Though most software development languages can be accessed entirely for free online, Codecademy's founders realized they needed to make the learning process more fun and engaging to achieve their objective. So they designed a system that allows people to take a course in any of dozens of programming languages, learning how to code step-by-step. Anyone can author a course for Codecademy, but each unit must adhere to certain guidelines—both for content and for gamey-ness. Users receive positive reinforcement throughout (mostly through badges), and they are regularly assessed (note: we didn't say *tested*) to ensure that they are learning the material.

What makes their design particularly compelling is that both the creators of these gamified lessons and the customers learning from them are part of a contiguous game environment that rewards participation. Creators, in particular, are scored on how well their students do and how many people use the approach. Refinement and novelty are both incentivized, giving lesson creators ample incentive to design a thoughtful grind, keep things fresh, tune rewards to the users, define progress, and stay engaged throughout.

Imagine if all modes of learning were designed in a tight loop between teachers and students. We've all been in a school setting where certain teachers were known as tough, and others as easy. But what if we could actually see the outcomes? And better still, what if teachers' performance then acted as a filter for deciding which students got to be in their classes? That's precisely the dynamic that Codecademy engages—and one that has delivered unprecedented results.

In other cases, the organization is the "teacher." Customers look up to a brand for knowledge, access, and progress. Whether you sell audiophile equipment or you offer tax services or public education—all of your customers are trying to learn and grow from their relationship with you. You can leverage the lessons of Codecademy to engage them and also to create bridges between employees and customers.

You can tie the performance of internal stakeholders to customer learning, and you can even make that connection transparent to your customers. For example, if you run a financial organization, make their literacy a key performance indicator for your organization. Measure this variable, and make their progress critical to your strategy. Then make it more fun: let your customers know who their teachers are—the team members directly responsible for their learning material. Let them form teams and compete to see who can do best on various measures of literacy or performance. As we illustrated in Part II, employees generally love meaningful, lighthearted competition—customers are no different. Connecting the two may produce exponential benefits.

Aiding in your customers' progression to mastery and supporting their educational goals will help engender long-term loyalty and engagement. But loyalty need not be a purely "selfless" act. If done well, leveraging the power of gamification, it can become a profit center in its own right.

Monetize Loyalty

If you are one of the 1.7 million people who flew in the United States today, you probably thought several things about the experience, none of which very likely included, "Wow, that was **fun!**"

Between the long lines, bad food, expensive fees, limited space, and cranky overworked employees, really what's there to enjoy? And that's all before considering that over 25 percent of flights are likely to be delayed or canceled. It's enough to earn airlines some of the worst customer satisfaction ratings of any industry. But what if there were some way to even the score? A way to get better service, get where you needed on time, and have fun doing it? Maybe you could play the game—and win instead of lose. Moreover, what if that game benefited both you and the companies involved in nearly equal measure?

If you already know how to play this game, you just might be a frequent flier. And if you're in the top 1 percent of fliers—known as "elites"—you drive as much as 25 percent of airline revenues. Your loyalty, it turns out, matters a lot. And one of the ways the airlines create and sustain engagement with you is by making the *game of travel* fun, complex, and "winnable."

In 2008 American Airlines implemented one of the first baggage fees by a legacy carrier. At the time, their wildly successful AAdvantage loyalty program was running out of ways to reward its over 80 million users. Suddenly a new prize was on the table: rack up the right amount of miles each year, and you never have to pay extra to travel with bags again. By 2010 a regular passenger was paying for amenities that were once taken for granted such as snacks, blankets, and pillows—but not the best fliers. *They* continued getting most of that for free, and then some. Every year since, carriers like American have tweaked their programs—always earning criticism and compliments. The goal: maximize fun and finances.

For travelers, it's play or be played. For the airlines, it's a game of life or death. After losing tens of billions of dollars in the decade following 2001, by 2012 U.S. airlines were reporting record profits. This was achieved in no small part by balancing the pain and pleasure in contemporary loyalty programs. Before 2001, loyalty programs were all about pleasure, offering continuous rewards for good behavior—for example, miles, upgrades, free flights, and great treatment. But they had become stagnant, and set against the backdrop of higher fuel prices and a global economic crisis, carriers had to radically rethink their approach. In short, they needed to rebalance the game.

They rose to the challenge, and the results of their efforts have been staggering.

In 2011 global airlines collected $22.6 billion in ancillary fees—charging ticket price add-ons like baggage charges, priority check-in charges, and seating fees. This was nearly double 2009's $13 billion fee haul, and it amounted to a healthy percentage of global airline revenues that had been nearly flat at just under $600 billion during that same time period. While these supplemental fees make up only 4 percent of airline sales, they are essentially responsible for the industry's profits. Total net income for airlines in 2011 was only $6.9 billion worldwide—a roughly 1 percent margin. U.S. carriers, originally resistant to this model, have become among its most ardent supporters. The country's largest carrier, United Airlines, collected $5 billion in fees—and Delta announced an intention to raise its fee haul by $1 billion to $3.5 billion by 2014.

Obviously, these fees have helped the airlines claw themselves back from the brink—becoming an undeniably lucrative part of their core business. At the same time, they've used this approach to strengthen their loyalty offering by waiving most of these charges for their most loyal fliers. Thus in a single stroke, airlines created a new point of friction out of thin air, and then they eliminated that speed bump for their most worthy consumers.

This change has recalibrated the loyalty equation, giving the game new challenges and impetus. It has also allowed the airlines to shift the discussion away from free flights and upgrades for all but the most elite fliers. After all, lower-tier customers now get a host of benefits (free bags! better seats!) that they didn't have before, so flight redemptions are less important. It has also allowed carriers to swell the ranks of their programs, by tens of millions of customers—often giving those tiers away in promotions or with credit cards, without devaluing the top tiers. Today, carriers like United have over 100 million frequent fliers, and the number continues to grow.

At the same time, loyalty programs have been increasing their focus on using online games to drive loyalty, blending tangible and intangible rewards in an effort to increase engagement and lower **costs**. One such game that made waves was United Airlines' *Optathlon*.

A healthy part of United's $5 billion in ancillary fees comes from selling "upgrades" to consumers. The company's research has shown, however, that unless you've experienced first-class travel, you're unlikely to shell out for their $99 to $600 upsell. Similarly, other upgrades (expedited handling, club access, and so on) require some exposure to get people interested. Needing a way to drive users to experience their premium products without simply giving them away, United turned to gamification.

The *Optathlon* was a series of games that could be played online or on your mobile device. Including titles such as *Legroom Legend*, *Line Jump Hero*, and *Mileage Ace*, each of the five games showcased one premium product. Users could play the games, learn about the products, and then take the game to the airport. During the prize period, fliers could play *Optathlon* at the airport to instantly unlock an upgrade or be entered into a $20,000 sweepstakes.

After a few months, the games blew away all expectations. Over 1 million fliers played them online, and 85,000 instant upgrades were given away at the airport. This, along with the immense press exposure for the game, delivered significant exposure for the United and its Mileage Plus program precisely when the airline needed it most. But its most exciting achievement happened after the sweepstakes ended. In the 12 months following the close of the prize period, over 4 million **additional** people played the *Optathlon* games, indicating that the fun of the game was not only in the prospect of winning but also in the engagement of the experience.

As these programs have matured, they have also come under increased scrutiny. From government to media, there is endless attention to the obvious details of these loyalty programs—redemptions, fees, and so on. But what's happening under the covers is even more interesting. Frequent-flier programs are generally highly profitable, even when the underlying airline is hemorrhaging money.

The reason is mileage sales. Every time you earn an airline mile—from your credit card, hotel stay, car rental, or mortgage refinance—the issuing company has paid that airline for those miles. Although mile purchase prices are not public, the consensus is that they cost approximately $0.01 in very large volumes (plus the U.S. government's 7.5 percent excise tax on miles). Major credit card companies, like Chase, Amex, and Citibank, buy and issue tens of billions of miles per year, generating at least $1 billion in revenue for American Airlines AAdvantage program alone.

These miles are then used for free flights and other, higher-margin redemptions (like magazine subscriptions or hotel stays). Still other miles—billions of them, in fact—expire every year in a process known as "breakage." By dramatically increasing the volume of mileage sales in the past decade and simultaneously increasing the margin on redemptions, airlines have been able to arbitrage the value of a mile and generate tremendous profits.

This is classic virtual economy design—much the same concept that drives big social games like *Farmville*. As frequent-flier programs and these games have evolved, they've learned from each other and improved their respective designs. In the case of large-scale loyalty programs, the game exists so that the company can sell its virtual currency (miles, points, credit, coins, and so on). This delivers a standalone revenue stream that allows loyalty to become a profit center and potentially a productized offering in itself.

Gamification is used throughout the programs to drive more usage and raise engagement. But again, for successful loyalty programs, the game is the thing. Over the next decade, there will be a significant consolidation and land grab for virtual currencies among customers. Much like the global currency markets, where almost every country has its own "coin of the realm," the same is true of gamified loyalty program providers. But as more and more companies discover the power of the method to drive engagement and revenue, there will be more currencies than users can handle.

While advanced virtual wallet systems will help consumers manage the clutter, there will nonetheless be demand for higher-quality currencies that are more convertible. Just as the U.S. dollar, euro, Japanese yen, British pound sterling, and Swiss franc are the real-world global currencies of record today, so too will a handful of virtual currencies be important to the customers of the future. And whoever's digital point system becomes the standard will have immense power—just as national governments do—to inflate or deflate its value and affect all the players in the ecosystem.

In this new, gamified race for the customer, where every organization has the potential to be Zimbabwe, the United States, or Switzerland, which will yours choose?

Sustained engagement is complex and fraught with distracting challenges. Once your organization accepts gamification and it begins to drive engagement throughout the consumer experience, you must choose to stay in it for the long haul in order to maintain momentum. By using the strategies laid out in this chapter, your company can join the ranks of world-class engagement pioneers to shape consumer behavior.

Once you are on your way sustaining customer engagement, you can use gamification to drive innovation and support through crowdsourcing techniques. This highly leveraged business strategy may enable you to turn gamification into an engine of creativity and profitability, based on your newly deepened customer relationships. That's a powerful opportunity that no company—regardless of industry—can afford to miss.

10

INNOVATING WITH CROWDSOURCING

For scientists working on ridding the world of HIV and AIDS, the past 30 years of the disease have been fraught with many failures and frustratingly slow discovery. Part of the challenge of curing HIV has been unmasking the virus itself, particularly understanding how it replicates and spreads within a host. The focus of researchers has therefore zeroed in on proteins—the so-called workhorses of our cells. The proteins in HIV—just like those in healthy cells—perform essential functions such as delivering nutrition, regulating key chemicals, and triggering replication. The hope is to develop therapies that can target and attack the virus on this level—stopping replication. Scientists also believe similar approaches could be used to conquer cancer and Alzheimer's disease—both of which are believed to be caused by problem proteins in our DNA.

However promising these therapies may be, they face a major and almost insurmountable hurdle: protein structures cannot be seen under a three-dimensional microscope. Although all proteins are composed of amino acids, each one has a distinct shape. And because proteins interact with other cellular elements much as a key fits into a lock, we need to clearly understand their structure to design therapies.

The way we do this is by *folding*—imagining the most efficient way to get all the amino acids together, with the correct shape, in three dimensions. It's not unlike assembling a highly complex three-dimensional jigsaw puzzle with millions of possible combinations, where the final shape looks nothing like a cube or square.

Software can be used to do this important work, but it requires extraordinary amounts of computing power to be effective. On the other hand, humans have an intuitive capacity to look at puzzles and figure out quickly how the pieces fit together in a visual space. This was an observation that the creators of Rosetta—a software solution for protein folding designed at the University of Washington—made while running one of their simulations. They found that researchers interacting with the software were frustrated when they would solve folding problems before the computer could. It seemed as though they easily noticed patterns that the software missed.

So they asked the obvious question: If people do this better than software, how can we get people to do the work? Thus was born *Foldit*—a gamified experience that teaches anyone how to fold proteins like a pro, using our innate ability to see three-dimensional patterns and find symmetry (Figure 10.1). The game explains the basic amino acids, the way they fit together, and the structural elements of proteins through a series of hands-on tutorial levels. Then, working alone and in teams from around the globe, you can apply your newfound skills to model, test, and share your hypotheses about protein structures for scientists. As the complexity of various proteins increases, so too does the amount of time required to solve the puzzle—in some cases, the effort required is measured in millions of workhours.

That was the case with *Foldit's* big headline-grabbing breakthrough. In 2011, 49,000 players began working on the structure of a key protein implicated in the fight against HIV. Scientists had spent the better part of the 15 years prior trying to decode this

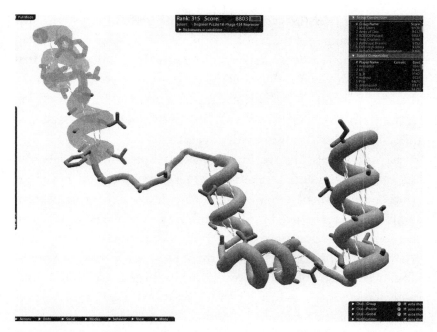

FIGURE 10.1 Folding proteins using the human intuition for three-dimensional spatial modeling is clearly shown in this image from the game *Foldit*.

enzyme—to no avail. However, after only 10 days, from Dakar to Moscow, the Internet cheered. *Foldit*'s players had solved the problem—figuring out the structure of the protein and bringing science a major step closer to finding the cure for the disease.

The breakthrough was momentous—both for the HIV research community and for the world at large. *Foldit* demonstrated that people are willing to work together for a common cause and use their shared human computational power to solve real problems. More important, *Foldit* also demonstrated that you don't need to dumb the problem down to get people to play: nearly 50 percent of the game's solvers had no formal math or science background.

So what made *Foldit* so successful at extracting complex labor from a group of people without compensation? Notably, players were given a chance to work on a problem of significance, with the right tools, and they were given a wide range of collaborators. But when the gamification elements were optimized, *Foldit* really took off. For example, the game includes scoring that shows you how you, your team, and the whole world are progressing—so you can easily see that your work makes a difference. It includes badges that give you positive reinforcement as you learn and work through the challenges. And to drive performance, it also includes competition in the form of leaderboards, enabling individuals to work against others on a team or an individual basis.

Beyond simply discovering the structure of proteins, *Foldit* also has another—potentially even more lucrative—purpose. Using the power of the crowd, it may be possible to design new proteins from scratch that can be used in the creation of new drugs, gene therapies, or other important medical applications. And while HIV and AIDS are obvious opportunities, there are a surprising number of similar problems of the same complexity in the world that don't easily lend themselves to algorithmic solutions. Many are even outside the scientific arena.

Foldit is a champion example of what is known as *crowdworking*, or more broadly, *crowdsourcing*. This strategy has exploded in popularity in recent years, as companies have taken to the crowd for everything from logos to product design, and from complex solutions to shared support and Q&A. Although it's not an entirely new idea, the rapid explosion of social technologies has made crowdsourcing a popular approach—even for major corporations with virtually limitless resources. This has propelled crowdsourcing to become a multi-billion-dollar industry in itself with far-reaching implications.

The unsung hero of the crowdsourcing movement is gamification. It is, after all, the dynamics of the game—its rewards, points, leaderboards, winners, and so on—that make it compelling. And structuring a winning crowdsourced experience is often more about the gamification design than the projects themselves. This is particularly—though by no means exclusively—true when there are insufficient resources to pay the full cost of labor.

In most crowdsourced services, we don't pay losers for their work—only winners. Just as Napoléon did with his Food Preservation Prize (as discussed in Chapter 1), we get to see a wide range of ideas but we pay as though we had only hired one person. The arbitrage between those two things is all about how the game is designed. In essence, in lieu of payment for their time, you are giving "players" an opportunity for greatness and notoriety, or perhaps just socialization and fun. Even if it does on its surface look like a mere "psychological reward," *Foldit* has been able to extract millions of workhours in free labor by offering players the chance to belong, make a significant contribution, socialize, and have fun. So, too, do most clever gamified crowdsourcing systems.

In this chapter we'll look at a few different approaches to leveraging the power of the crowd through the lens of how gamification accomplishes or provides the following:

> ➤ Changes in behavior
> ➤ Reductions in costs and improvements in quality
> ➤ Inspiration for innovation and ideation
> ➤ Inspiration for new product development

Changing Behavior

Those who contributed to *Foldit* saw scientific progress as valuable to humanity and ultimately to the individual. This value was derived from the success of each contributor's action and is in fact the motivating factor behind why people choose to play in the first place—though the gamification elements are what keep them there (and coming back).

One of the most widely embraced examples of crowdsourcing is Wikipedia, the world's sixth-most-popular website. This online encyclopedia features collaborative information gathering on a multilingual and international scale, and it is used regularly by over 350 million people. It has grown to include more than 23 million unique articles written and edited by as many as 100,000 individual volunteers. While the articles are vetted, depending on which of the 285 distinct language sites you are visiting, edits are often immediately visible, errors and all. Launched in 2001, Wikipedia has rapidly displaced traditional encyclopedias as the go-to resource for research.

Behind Wikipedia's success is a looming threat, however: as the site has grown and matured, the pace of participation has declined precipitously. Whereas the site used to add as many as 10,000 new editors per month, in recent years those numbers have been on the decline by nearly double. Over time, this will leave an impossibly small group of individuals to curate the world's largest information resource, likely leading to inaccuracies, atrophy, and permanent decline.

The reason? Wikipedia has failed to gamify. Neil Robertson, founder of crowdsourcing platform *Trada*, identified seven kinds of motivation that drive crowdsourced behavior, including cash, points, leaderboards, badges, reputation, community, and collaboration. Within this scope, Wikipedia leverages only community and collaboration, leaving the other drivers out of the equation. If Wikipedia introduces more game mechanics, it could create more sustainable user interest and bring in a wider editing audience.

In an ideal world, everyone would contribute to Wikipedia. The founders envisioned a communal resource that served the world's need for knowledge by leveraging everyone's basic desire to share what he or she knows. Today, control of this knowledge is concentrated in the hands of a few editors. With its constant fundraising appeals, it's not hard to imagine Wikipedia transforming into a cross between a PBS station and a commercial encyclopedia. However, by leveraging game mechanics, the site could incite major behavior change: getting people to impart what they know in exchange for an experience that rewards them with fun and the recognition of their peers.

This goal—of making a major change in customers' entrenched behaviors—is not as far-fetched as it sounds. The harder that change is to achieve, the better gamification seems to perform. Take, for example, speeding.

Since England hung its first speed limit sign (10 miles per hour) in 1861, drivers around the world have been "encouraged" by the government to maintain a safe driving speed. And it was probably in 1861 that the first driver exceeded the posted speed limit. Since then, commuters and legislators have waged a battle on the roadways, ratcheting up enforcement (and revenues to the state) through a series of human and technological advancements (for example, radar and speed cameras). As cars have gotten faster, so too has the pace of speed limit enforcement.

Interestingly, speed limits appear to have little impact on people's behavior. In real-world studies, as changes to the speed limit in developed nations are leveled, how fast a driver will actually go is minimally—if at all—affected. For example, in one U.K. test where speed limits were reduced from 60 to 40 miles per hour, the average driver's speed declined only 4 miles per hour. In the United States, across 22 states, speed limits were reduced in increments of 5 to 15 miles per hour, and drivers showed no reduction in speed whatsoever. In fact, the National Motorists Association found that speed limits and the threat of fines alone had no discernible effect on 227 specific locations studied across the United States.

So it seems that drivers are unmoved by the portent of superior tracking technology and increasingly heavy fines. Speeding has therefore become a highly *entrenched* behavior that is very resistant to change. Although people know the potential risks and penalties if they get into an accident or are caught, most drivers have the delusional belief that they are better behind the wheel or better at avoiding detection than everyone around them. In the face of this intransigence, and despite spending billions to achieve safer roads, authorities have simply resigned themselves to a perpetual game of cat and mouse.

Now a new solution has emerged, based on the principles of gamification, that has shaken our thinking about what to do with inveterate speeders. It's called *Speed Camera Lottery*, and it has done something no one thought possible: lowered speeds in a way that drivers actually like.

In 2010 Volkswagen launched a gamified ad campaign called *Fun Theory* designed to encourage players to come up with gamified solutions to some of the world's problems. Kevin Richardson, a well-respected game designer and producer, proposed *Speed Camera Lottery*. The concept, which was one of the prize winners, made use of the existing antispeed cameras set up throughout Stockholm—Sweden's largest city. The cameras were modified, and a new interaction was introduced that could change how we think about speeding.

The premise was simple: drivers at one of Stockholm's busiest intersections had their speeds and license plates recorded by a marked camera. Those who broke the speed limit were fined, and the money from the fines was pooled for a prize pot. Those who drove at or below the speed limit were entered into a lottery to win that prize pot. They received one lottery ticket every time they compliantly passed by the camera (with a maximum number of passes allowed per day). Over the test period, *Speed Camera Lottery* showed a 22 percent decrease in the average driving speed. By switching the emphasis from punishment-based incentives to reward-based incentives—or from legal regulations to the rules of a game—the *Speed Camera Lottery* accomplished in three days what 150 years of driving regulations could not, and it allowed people to have fun while doing it.

Beyond its broad behavior change importance, drivers' reactions to the *Speed Camera Lottery* can serve as an interesting case study for motivating customer behavior. In so many aspects of their lives, from government to commercial interactions, customers are given little reward for good behavior but lots of punishment for bad—even simple, entrenched ideas like credit card payment penalties, product refund deadlines, or cable restrictions on certain TV programs. In almost every case, the penalties serve important business purposes—but they don't give customers a pathway to a positive alternative. The best people can hope for is an avoidance of punishment.

The more ways you can reward customers in positive ways—even, say, by congratulating them for making their credit card payments on time for six months in a row—the better they will feel about themselves and your underlying product or service. This will also set the stage for engaging them in other activities—from customer service to feedback exchanges—that are increasingly important in today's competitive economy. Your customers, it turns out, are willing to work with and for you, if given the right incentives, rewards, and fun.

Customer Service and Community: Reducing Costs and Improving Quality

Building a great, vibrant, and collaborative community is a challenge—even with plenty of resources at your disposal. But when your company is a start-up, and your target audience is made up of fiercely independent and misanthropic software developers, the challenge is even greater. Moreover, if you set the goal of getting the cream of the crop to participate, it can seem insurmountable.

In Chapter 2's case study of StackOverflow and StackExchange, we began to wade into this territory. To recap: the company was founded in 2008 as a community in which developers could answer each other's questions (Figure 10.2). It was the brainchild of Jeff Attwood. Having seen other large-scale Q&A websites like Yahoo! Answers, however, Attwood understood that a system designed to incentivize action—at any cost—would likely produce a lot of superfluous and nonuseful content. This was the biggest problem for Yahoo! Answers, a Q&A website with over 200 million users at its peak. Although easy to dismiss today, Yahoo! Answers once counted academics, politicians, authors, and many great thinkers among its users.

Attwood, who had grown up around video games, focused on a single truism that would guide the design of his now famous platform:

"Reputation always comes from your peers. It doesn't come from the system."

Attwood understood that this dynamic was at the heart of how to scale and measure the success of individuals participating in

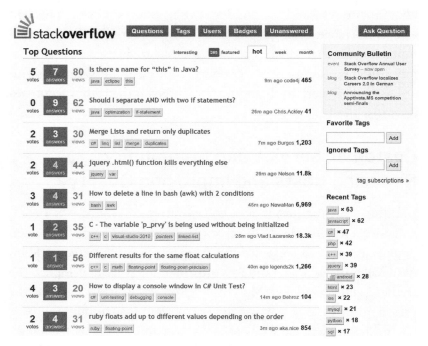

FIGURE 10.2 StackOverflow, a collaborative Q&A environment for software developers, makes extensive use of gamified reputation to drive performance.

a Q&A environment—and in any peer support context, for that matter. So he designed StackOverflow around a reputation system driven mostly by peer behavior. That is, others vote to determine your reputation, which is expressed by rank and score. For example, you can't even vote for something on the site until you have been voted on by someone else. The site tracks votes broadly in the form of a virtual point system (reputation points, known colloquially as "creds"), and it awards users badges for special achievements. Some of its badges (which can be acquired both digitally and physically) are so rare that user discussion forums are rife with legends and stories about how to get one.

While all of this is exciting in its own right, what really makes StackOverflow so impressive is both *who* is using the system and *what* they are doing with it. The 1 million or so developers on the site are among the top experts in their fields. These are folks who sometimes earn hundreds or thousands of dollars for their technical expertise, who are online helping each other solve detailed technical problems *for free*. In this environment they don't charge, and StackOverflow makes no effort to reward them with cash of any kind from the inside. The premise is that users help each other, and in the process they establish credibility. This gives the participants a win in real life, an opportunity to move through (and "win," if they choose) at a new status system, and the chance to give back. In other words, there is a lot of emotional value to participating.

What the game allows the site to do is to aggregate this expertise and arbitrage it by selling advertising and other services against that effort. In a sense, the crowd's work generates the inventory for further monetization. And because of its quality emphasis, the site has been able to make it successful with a fraction of the traffic of Yahoo! or Quora (another Q&A site). The company has raised $18 million to help it pursue its vision, and it has taken the actual design of StackOverflow's gamified system and turned that into a web service: StackExchange. This new offering can be leveraged for vertical communities using the same pattern—over 85 of them at last count.

Although the examples of transforming a company or industry through gamification are many, few have had the cultural or business impact of Kickstarter. Started in 2009 with a mission to democratize fund-raising for artistic and business projects, Kickstarter has become the king of crowdsourced funding. Today, anyone with a great product, movie, game, book, company, or other idea can create a description, embed a video, and put it up on Kickstarter to solicit funds. There, millions of people from around the world view, comment, share, and invest in projects of all kinds. By the fourth quarter of 2012, the site had helped 72,000 projects raise over $370 million, of which 13 individual ideas raised $1 million or more.

At the heart of what makes Kickstarter work is the exposure to great ideas and the power of socializing those concepts. But gamification plays a significant role in driving both funders and projects to the platform. For example, Kickstarter uses an all-or-nothing mechanic: if you don't raise the minimum amount required by your deadline, you don't get any of the funds pledged. This approach ensures that investors feel confident the project will at least be able to get off the ground. Further, the site prominently displays critical stats about each project (dollars raised, timeline, number of funders, and so on) along with leaderboards that let everyone see how each opportunity is trending against others.

But it is the rewards system that really makes the site unique. Because of U.S. laws restricting equity sales in private companies, Kickstarter projects cannot offer stock in exchange for investment. Therefore, the site forces its participants to find alternate "rewards" to give investors, handily demonstrating the ability of status, access, and power—or nonmonetary benefits—to drive behavior. Generally, investors are tiered based on how much they give each project, and rewards differ based on the level of investment.

Let's take, as an example, Charlie Kaufman's *Anomalisa* film project on Kickstarter, which raised $406,000 (or double its $200,000 goal) and has been one of the most successful projects on the site. Kaufman, the creator of popular cult movies such as *Being John Malkovich, Adaptation,* and *Eternal Sunshine of the Spotless Mind,* took to Kickstarter to fund a stop-motion animation project he was particularly passionate about. Of the 5,770 backers, contributors of $5 or more received a thank you on the movie's Facebook page, contributors of $20 or more got a digital download of the film (2,297 investors), and contributors of $300 or more got a signed hoodie. Ante up $2,500 and you had the choice of either a Skype chat or drinks on the town with the movie's producers. And for $10,000, you would receive all the goodies and executive producer credit in the film itself—a tier in which five individuals participated (and was sold out almost immediately).

Notably, none of the tiers offered "points" or cash stemming from any commercial success of the film. Although some of the offered rewards could wind up costly in dollars (like buying and shipping hundreds of sweatshirts) or time (like potentially having to share an evening of drinks with someone painfully boring), none even comes close to the typical expense of profit sharing. And from the backers' standpoint, many of the benefits were so rare and meaningful (a signed copy of one of the sets!) that they were more valuable to true fans than cash from revenue sharing would be. Even the opportunity to participate in a Charlie Kaufman film project was sufficient to motivate some of the key investors to action. And from an advertising standpoint, the emotional investment of 5,770 people also meant a built-in audience when the film is finally released.

Kickstarter's success handily illustrates a key point about gamification and the crowd: you can get people to do extraordinary things together—often economically irrational things—if you provide the right feedback, friends, and fun. You need not offer cash rewards, as long as people are getting the right psychological benefits (reputation, connection, contribution) from their participation. And nowhere can this irrational action be seen more clearly than in innovation and ideation.

Inspiring Innovation and Ideation

Beyond scientific discovery and community building, gamification can also be a critical strategy when turning to the crowd for innovation and idea generation. Just as with most of the examples shared thus far, recognition (or status) plays a critical role in making this model work.

As a company that knows a thing or two about recognition, InnoCentive was founded in 2001 to advance the use of grand challenges to solve problems in life sciences, industry, and more. Today, over 170,000 experts in a range of industries are part of the InnoCentive network, helping organizations of all sizes drive innovation through prize-linked challenges ranging in value from $10,000 to $1 million.

The InnoCentive model is based on the same kind of grand challenges that have been used to solve problems in food preservation, trans-Atlantic crossings, and commercial space flight. Effectively, it is a first-past-the-post contest that rewards one winner with a large prize for his or her success. But an interesting dynamic exists within most grand challenges, and InnoCentive is no exception: frequently the prize doesn't justify the effort.

Let's take an example from a typical InnoCentive challenge to understand this behavior. In 2012, the famed Cleveland Clinic asked the InnoCentive community of online solvers to help it figure out a way to reconnect two pieces of human tissue without using sutures. Over 800 people signed on to solve the problem, which would pay up to $30,000 for a theoretical solution that would be licensed to the clinic in a perpetual and exclusive way—so the solver would lose all rights to the idea going forward. Given the huge economic potential for such a solution—especially in surgeries involving fluid transport tissues—why would someone sign away his or her rights for a small fraction of its potential economic value?

The answer belies the extraordinary power of crowdsourced innovation challenges—that the recognition for solving the problem is far more valuable to the solver than the money. Solvers may engage to seek the recognition of their peers, to challenge themselves to a personal best, or even to look for a job. But no matter what, if they have the skills to solve the problem (and indications are that at least one solution should suffice for the Cleveland Clinic), they are not getting the full value of their work. In fact, InnoCentive provides extensive advice to its seeker community on the appropriate pricing, no doubt gleaned from the tens of thousands of contests launched. In almost every case the solution trades at a significant discount to its value—and there can be only one winner.

There are four factors that drive this arbitrage: the credibility of the InnoCentive platform, the perception of the brand seeking the solution, the public scale of the problem, and the competition among solvers. Although InnoCentive brings new ideas to market in a startlingly efficient way, the net effect of this market is to lower the price of solutions stemming from novel challenges. Today, solvers do not compete to offer the lowest price (as they might in other marketplaces), but why pay a university or consultancy's inflated costs to do basic research? The lesson: the more "noncash" opportunities you can provide (job, fame, recognition, and so on), the more likely people are to trade down in terms of economic value to be the winner of your challenge.

But what about when the challenge is much less defined and more about process than outcomes? IBM's *Innov8*—an open software platform we introduced in Chapter 2—was designed to let players understand, model, and learn about business processes. IBM believes that even a slight increase in process improvement can result in margin improvement, increased capacity, and a reduction in required employees or capital. Since launching in 2008, *Innov8* has been a smashing success for IBM, and today over 1,000 educational institutions and corporations use it to teach the fundamentals of business process management (BPM) to aspiring process engineers and leaders at all levels of the organization.

In *Innov8*, users pass through the basics of BPM using either a real or completely invented experience. There, they can explore and model how the process works and discover how the pieces fit together. Then they collaborate on different models and explore what-if scenarios. Through emulation of customer service, traffic flow, and supply chain models, *Innov8* allows users to focus on specific BPM problems and solutions. By making the processes visual, interactive, and social, the app lets laypeople and experts reset their knowledge and interact in new and unique ways.

Now, groups of users can collaborate and solve process issues using *Innov8*. For example, IBM's *CityOne*—a real-world process simulation game based on its *SmartPlay Framework*—is being used to develop real-world solutions to urban planning issues. As tens of thousands of people play *CityOne*, they collaborate to solve problems like how to increase the water supply, ensure adequate transportation, and expand governmental representation during a city's growth. It's like the famous simulation game *SimCity*, but it is for actual urban planners who can use the data to optimize an actual city. Similarly, *Innov8*'s BPM modules are used by students, academics, and experts around the world to tackle real-world problems.

Obviously, the need for business process engineering is something that most industries face at one time or another. The clever use of advanced design and gamification constructs has allowed IBM to turn this demand into a significant market asset, and one with an established track record of powerful innovation behind it. It actually works!

Part of what makes *Innov8* so compelling is the simple truism that it's significantly more fun than the alternative (pen and paper or flat, custom software modeling options). By bringing fun and game mechanics to what otherwise ranged from boring to impenetrable, *Innov8* has changed companies and lives.

But what if fun is an implicit part of the experience, rather than explicit? Can gamification be used with crowdsourcing to actually replace or supplement the work of staff members who are core to the business operation? That's precisely what some leading organizations have been able to achieve.

Driving New Product Development

Most people know CNN as the first channel in the world devoted to 24-hour news coverage. Since its launch in 1980, CNN and its affiliate networks (HLN, Airport, and CNN International, to name a few) have redefined the news gathering and dissemination industry. Despite suffering a substantial ratings decline in recent years, the channel still runs a major, traditional news gathering operation—with over 36 bureaus scattered among dozens of countries. In these locations, CNN reporters do the traditional—and labor-intensive—job of tracking down leads, chasing scoops, driving trucks, setting up satellite uplinks, and broadcasting the news as it happens. This is augmented by an extensive online news gathering and reporting presence at CNN.com that also leverages news channels like the Associated Press (AP) for syndication.

But beyond their traditional news approach, CNN has innovated on the use of the crowd for news. Augmenting their thousands of regular media staffers are 950,000 iReporters—citizen journalists empowered by CNN to gather news with the channel as their distribution system. Launched in 2008, *iReport* leveraged the advent of widely available video camera phones and the hunger for "news streams" that were becoming popular on Twitter and Facebook. The company sought to allow anyone who was near a story to tell it.

CNN's innovation has led to millions of stories being filed, with iReporters frequently bringing classified or insider scoops to the network. The power of video and Internet connectivity that now exists almost everywhere allows stories, however crude, to be uploaded from just about anywhere, any time. Since its launch, *iReport* has scooped a number of events, including the Virginia Tech shooting, the 2004 tsunami, the 7/7 bombings in London, and the collapse of the I-35 bridge in Minnesota. In each case CNN was able to get notable video and audio footage hours—and sometimes days—before regular news outlets were able to get traditional teams into place.

No one questions whether or not the iReporters are able to replace classic news approaches. Rather, the most powerful dynamic about *iReport* is that CNN effectively outsources some portion of its news gathering to individuals whom they do not pay. Instead of offering cash compensation, iReporters are able to earn a series of badges, awards at an annual awards event, and—most importantly—the opportunities to have their iReports used on the news or on the home page of CNN.com. Additionally, users get a chance to express themselves and to tell their stories in an open and unvarnished way.

This exposure opportunity—the chance to be seen, or get fame, combined with the expressive power of the video medium—is so strong that users need not be compensated at all for their effort. The company is able to scale because the game and its reward model are designed well enough to drive user engagement over the long term. The combination of these ideas is very powerful indeed.

But not all gamified, crowdsourced approaches to work and product development lack cash compensation. In fact, one of the most interesting start-ups in the physical product space embraces cash compensation as a core part of its strategy for driving excellence and engagement in its community.

Quirky, founded in 2009 in New York, is a new kind of product manufacturer—a social one. Bringing together the crowd on its website, Quirky allows individuals to collaborate on the ideation, optimization, marketing, and sales of new products. It starts with individuals proposing products they would like to see made—for example, the PivotPower, which is a $30 flexible power strip that can go around objects. It has sold over 370,000 units to date. The crowd then votes on the products, offering refinements and suggestions to improve them. Once products receive a certain number of votes and peer support, the products become eligible to get made— and then the creator and contributors continue to refine them. If the company elects to manufacture the products, then participants become part of the marketing and distribution concept as well.

The core idea is that the crowd can leverage its unique order-from-chaos ability to define and then highlight those products that most need to get made. By eliciting a large number of participants, the company can also identify what the market scope and target audience can be, and the refinements are used to optimize the products for marketing and production.

Probably the most interesting twist in Quirky is the way that the company divides revenue with the community. Effectively, everyone's participation is tracked and graded by the system and each other. Based on how much you contribute to the process of getting the product designed, refined, made, and sold, you are given a "share" of its net proceeds. Thus 30 percent of direct sales and 10 percent of channel sales are shared with the community, of which 35 percent are reserved for the inventor. The rest is split among participants, in increments as low as 0.1 percent.

Interestingly, all of the participants who meet a certain minimum contribution level—including those who don't merit a rev-

Innovation can get pretty quirky, pretty quickly. Check out some of the best customer innovation concepts at *The Gamification Revolution app, downloadable at* http://gamrev.com—where you will find videos, social links, and innovative ways to read, share, and discuss this book with your friends and colleagues.

enue share—are listed in a product's brochure included with the sale. Not dissimilar to the credits that roll at the end of a film or TV show, this approach allows for a wide range of associate producers to get their names on particular projects for various kinds of contributions—making it more likely that more people will participate. Additionally, users can earn revenue for social selling, giving a project an aspect of multilevel marketing taken to a whole new level.

Fundamentally, Quirky is trying to decrease the risks in new product development. By engaging the crowd in a game to get a product made, using a scoring system to gauge participation at all levels of the life cycle—from design to sales—Quirky is aligning incentives from inventor to market. Quirky then gets to benefit from this intellectual capital without returning any cash to users until well after the first product revenues have been received.

In fact, Quirky makes inventors pay $10 just to submit an idea. This kind of "basic commitment" mechanic ensures that Quirky minimizes chaff submissions without merit—weeding out those who don't believe $10 worth in their concept. The whole value chain has yet to prove its financial mettle—the company is still private—but Quirky has raised $23 million and lots of great social media buzz for its products. Using gamified crowdsourcing, Quirky is well on its way to fundamentally changing the cost-staffing model for product development organizations.

Overall, the use of crowdsourcing and crowdwork to change the economics of intellectual capital is an unstoppable force. As companies realize that they can realistically use the crowd to solve customer service issues, drive innovation, do on-the-ground work, and even design and build new products, the possibilities are endless. At the heart of each of these is gamification at work. The power of the game designs and mechanics—from points and badges to epic quests and fun—enables this transformative approach to take root. As you've seen in the examples, when a gamified crowdsourced system becomes successful, the game quickly becomes the focus. It is critical for your organization to embrace that dynamic sooner rather than later. In this way, you can lead the gamification revolution with the support of all your troops—even the crowdsourced ones.

GAMIFY YOUR READ

Socialize Your Read

What's the biggest problem facing you at work? Collaborate with a colleague and together design a gamified solution to that problem. In 400 words or less, post your solution on *The Gamification Revolution* app, and get feedback on your idea from the gamification community—and a chance to win direct feedback from a gamification expert!

11

IN CONCLUSION

★

The kids of today are changing the world of tomorrow. Over the last five years major strides have been made in curing cancer and solving the world's environmental crisis, all by teenagers competing in high school science fairs. In 2008 a 16-year-old named Daniel Burd from Waterloo, Canada, came up with a proposal for a safe, fast, and effective way to biodegrade plastics. In 2012 there were two major strides made in the fight against cancer: Angela Zhang, a 17-year-old, developed what she calls "a Swiss army knife for cancer," which is being touted as a potential cure, while 15-year-old Jack Andraka found what seems to be a breakthrough in the way we detect pancreatic cancer. The simple blood test he proposes will easily and effectively offer warning signs during the disease's earliest stages.

But ask today's managers and marketers about this millennial generation—and you're likely to hear an entirely different story. Words like "oversensitive," "ambitionless," "lazy," "distracted," and "entitled" are thrown around to describe this group. Though it's not the only cause, games have played a big role in driving these personalities—creating a group of 150 million people who think faster, more technologically, and just *differently* than the generations that came before them. But if you listened to the complaints of managers, teachers, and pundits, you might get the impression that this generation will never amount to anything and they just aren't worth the effort.

But maybe they are actually teaching us an important lesson. Our prevailing methods of chastising, motivating, teaching, and engaging them are the *wrong way*. We are moving rapidly toward a future where "fun" is the new "work." Fun is also the new buying, selling, attention grabbing, and health achieving. In an age when personal satisfaction trumps monetary wealth, ensuring happiness, fulfillment, and enjoyment in your workplace among your employees and your customers is becoming the rule rather than the exception. Gamification is leading the charge to radically change industries by making it *more fun* and ultimately more effective at building a strong, happy, and better engaged community.

Gartner Group says that by 2015, 70 percent of the world's largest companies will be using gamification. And by that same year, hundreds of thousands of start-ups, nonprofits, and governmental organizations will also be leveraging the best ideas from games, loyalty programs, and behavioral economics to drive attention, engagement, and results.

Whether you're focusing on employees or customers, gamification continues to produce unprecedented results for three principal reasons:

1. Gamification is the language of this new generation.
2. The benefits of gamification apply equally well to older stakeholders.
3. Gamification delivers affordable, measurable, and scalable behavior change.

And while gamification may seem edgy or complex today, no doubt there are already pockets of expertise inside your organization (both internal and customer facing) that are using or thinking about using gamification right now. What they need in order to drive the company to the next level is a clear strategy that makes engagement a priority. By seeing the potential of gamification now, your vision will help the organization adapt to a future in which fun, engagement, and reward aren't optional—they're required. From automobiles to finance, government to education, the number of examples of industries in which a tectonic shift is under way—driven by social, mobile, and gamelike technologies—is immense.

Gamification itself can even be used to develop these future strategies. From the earliest days of scenario planning in the postwar era to today's global, crowdsourced strategy competitions, game concepts have played a critical role in predicting the future for organizations. While gamification isn't new in strategic planning, an increasing focus on making the process itself fun and rewarding, while raising the abilities of those involved, has made the gamification of strategy more important than ever. This trend extends even to those employees not involved in the strategic process directly, which makes the need for enhanced training, development, and performance improvement greater than ever.

But finding and retaining those key players is tough. Despite a challenging economy, 31 percent of small businesses report major obstacles in finding qualified workers, according to the *Wall Street Journal* and Vistage International. And white-collar skills aren't the only ones being sought—41 percent of the manufacturing industry can't find qualified workers, while 30 percent in the service industry say the same. Meanwhile, 29 percent of retail sector companies are facing increased challenges when looking for employees to move into jobs without extensive (and expensive) training. Gamification changes the game in recruitment by helping to surface the best candidates quickly, extending the pre-employment testing regime to core skills, and making recruitment more social.

The challenge in recruitment is rising, in large part due to the fact that employee retention isn't what it used to be. The average company can expect to lose anywhere from 20 to 50 percent of its employee base each year. CareerBuilder.com reports that 76 percent of all employees would leave their current position if the right opportunity came along. Meanwhile, in the spring of 2012, MetLife released its tenth annual survey of employee trends and attitudes in which it reported that employee loyalty rates were at a seven-year low. In fact, MetLife said that one in three employees reported an intention to leave his or her job by the end of the year.

The reasons for this employee malaise are widely disputed, but one thing is sure: people who are happy don't want to leave, while people who are unhappy do. It's that simple. Further, employees who feel purposeful and connected to their work—getting feedback, working with their friends, and having fun—work harder, longer, and better.

According to CareerBliss.com, of the top 10 companies reporting the happiest employees, 8 openly use gamified practices with their workforce.

The list of the "Happiest Companies in the World":

10. Chevron: Incentive packages and employees club
9. Ericsson: Brand ambassador program
8. Fidelity Investments
7. The U.S. Air Force: Well-known badges and leveling
6. Centex
5. BASF: Cultural and sports activities
4. Nordstrom: A sense of personal agency
3. Johnson & Johnson: Maintaining employee health
2. Fluor: Business simulations
1. Hilton Worldwide: *Unreal Engine 3 Simulation*

At the same time, many thousands more companies have reinvented their performance feedback systems using new gamified approaches that deliver instant, social rewards and recognition for a job well done. Set against this context, it's also no wonder that many of these top-performing companies have gamified their employee health and wellness programs too. By making fitness programs part of the workplace, employers have activated collaboration and competition in ways that drive culture, morale, and cohesion.

And it's not just the employees and internal stakeholders who are empowered by gamification. It's customers as well. As the level of noise and distraction in the market increases, so too have businesses' desperate attempts at grabbing customer attention. People have an almost limitless set of choices to fill their spare time—all available instantly at their fingertips. Whereas they used to give a new store, experience, or website three to five minutes to prove itself, today's customer has less than 60 seconds to spare. At the same time, activities that used to be considered distractions in themselves—like watching television—are now experienced with a second or *third* screen nearly 25 percent of the time. Apparently, we need to distract ourselves from all that "great" programming on the tube.

This same need for additional stimulation and engagement— once again driven by millennial exposure to games—also creates a unique opportunity. If you can use gamification to cut through the noise, you can get unprecedented connection and dialogue. You can do this by leveraging a wide range of game mechanics, including surprise and delight. Most important though, you must be where the users are—gamify the second (and third) screens if you must, and own the distraction instead of fighting it.

Once you've got your customer's attention, you can amplify it using the power of social connection, progression to mastery, and viral loops. These gamified dynamics must be constantly tested, measured, and refined to optimize the experience for what the consumer needs. And it's critical to never let it get boring; even the best games can lose steam if you don't keep them fresh. If you are successful at maintaining engagement with gamification, you can parlay that into a new-style loyalty program that minimizes tangible rewards, instead paying out in *status, access,* and *power.* The best examples have even managed to monetize this concept, turning loyalty points into a profit center and jousting for dominance in a strategic global market for virtual currency.

Customers who are engaged and aligned with your brand vision can do even more. With the right incentives, you can get the crowd to design products, solve problems, and create intellectual property that you can monetize. This concept, called *crowdsourcing,* has yielded major solutions to science, economic, and creative problems. This proves that you can even get lower-skilled customers to do hard work and solve real problems without having to shy away from the tough stuff. If everyone is aligned, properly incentivized, and enjoying themselves, the sky's the limit.

And it really is.

Whether you manufacture widgets or deliver services, your employees are young, old, or a mix, the power of gamification can transform your organization. The key is to seize the moment and drive your company's strategy now while the market is rife with opportunity and the future is yet to be written. With a shift this big, the last thing you want to do is get left behind.

As the examples have highlighted in this book, forward-thinking organizations of all sizes are changing the world by capitalizing on this intersection of games, loyalty programs, and behavioral economics. They all share one source of optimism: a belief that human behavior can be changed through good, engaging design. As these examples—and the hundreds more that didn't make it into the book—prove, it can be done.

In 1982 John Seward Johnson II erected an iconic sculpture of a bronze businessman sitting on a bench across from the World Trade Centers in New York City. After the 2001 destruction of those buildings, a restored statue was placed in Zuccotti Park at the bottom of Wall Street. On a sunny summer day in 2012, a little girl holding onto her mother's hand stood in front of the statue. As she peered over the top of the statue's open briefcase lid, she turned a curious face up to her mother and asked, "What's that?"

The mother replied, smiling sheepishly at several passersby, "That's a calculator. It's how people used to add numbers in the olden days."

"Well, what's that?" the child asked.

"That's a letter opener." The little girl blinked blankly so her mother continued. "People used to get e-mail in paper envelopes, so they had to open a lot of them, and it hurt their fingers."

"Oh," the little girl nodded.

They inspected several more items until finally the little girl stood quietly looking thoughtfully at the statue. Then she reached into her mother's pocket and pulled out a touch screen mobile device and set it down inside the briefcase.

"He looks like he needs it," she explained to her surprised mother, shrugging her little shoulders.

As she walked away, the mother picked up the gadget and shook her head in wonder as she followed the child onto the crowded sidewalk.

Bronze is pretty good. But as any achiever will tell you, gold is the only color that matters.

—New York, New York
   January 2013
   @gzicherm
   @joselinder

By now, you've probably completed all the challenges at http://gam rev.com with *The Gamification Revolution* social app. Just in case you haven't, it's not too late to check out the videos, notes, social media lists, and cavalcade of website addresses in the app—and to share this book with your best friends and colleagues.

GAMIFY YOUR READ ANSWER KEY

CHAPTER 1

Chapterwide Scavenger Hunt

- ➤ Nicolas Appert won Napoléon's Food Preservation Prize.
- ➤ Devotees of the McDonald's *Monopoly* game claim they will:
  - ◆ Travel to find McDonald's outside of their neighborhoods.
  - ◆ Visit McDonald's more often.
  - ◆ Increase the size of their orders even if they are not hungry for the extra food.
- ➤ Social games developer Zynga is everyone's biggest competitor according to this chapter.
- ➤ According to a 2009 study, 60 percent of people in the western world play computer and/or video games on a regular basis.
- ➤ The average gamer is a 43-year-old woman.
- ➤ A Common Sense Media (CSM) study showed that 23 percent of five- to eight-year-olds use more than one technology medium at a time.

➤ In order to bring progression to mastery into your organization in a meaningful way, you must first design the key mechanics.
➤ Meaningful game mechanics are mentioned throughout this chapter and include:
  ◆ Points
  ◆ Badges
  ◆ Prizes and other rewards
  ◆ Social reinforcement
  ◆ Challenges
  ◆ Goals
  ◆ Markers toward the goals

For more answers we might have missed, visit *The Gamification Revolution* app!

CHAPTER 2

Questions and Answers

Q What does eBay's feedback score indicate about a seller?
A Trustworthiness

Q The focus of the chief engagement officer is to drive, what?
A Engagement

Q Chamillionaire uses his game *Chamillitary* to harness the energy of his, what?
A Fans

Q The SAP community network is designed to connect whom?
A Clients

CHAPTER 3

Riddle Me This!

Q What atmospheric condition uses thunder, lightning, and heavy rains in formulating fun?
A Gamestorming

CHAPTER 4

Choose Your Own Adventure—Solve Target's Check Out Problem Yourself!

Solution 1: Because the work of your checkout team has been sluggish and causing severe backups, you decide to motivate the staff by promising a pizza party after work one day in exchange for a little pep and faster service.

Results of Solution 1: Initially the staff members are excited about the weekly pizza party, and their work may or may not reflect it. However, over time the "reward" becomes an expectation, and the staff members return to their old sluggish ways. Because the reward isn't tied to specific behaviors, the power of its efficacy is limited.

Solution 2: You decide to punish your checkout team members for their poor performance by cutting five minutes off of their break time. You let all of them know that they are on probation and that if things don't pick up in line, they can expect to be replaced.

Results of Solution 2: Some team members attempt to make the changes you seek; however, the majority become angry. The backlash is swift as some people quit, dissatisfied and frustrated, while others refuse to pick up the pace and instead allow their work to fall off even further. As you increase punishment in accordance with the bad behavior of your staff members, the dissatisfaction on all sides continues to grow.

Solution 3: You want to help your checkout staff members rally so you offer a weekly prize in the form of a $20 gift card for the individual who consistently gets the most customers through the checkout process in three minutes or less. Using the clock on the checkout computer, employees track their work by printing out a receipt at the end of each transaction

Results of Solution 3: Your staff members' behavior quickly shifts as they become players in your game. Over time games within the game form, with staff members competing against their friends and superiors. Employee satisfaction increases as does customer satisfaction. By adding surprises and twists over time, your staff members stay invested in the game and continue to play it, and they maintain the positive behavior it sets up.

CHAPTER 6

Timed Read

"Like Flies to Honey: Making Recruitment Fun"

Q What company used a puzzle on a billboard to attract new recruits?
A Google

True or false Quixey's challenge had more than 100 winners.
A False

Q Winners of the first challenge in this section of the chapter were told that they were some of the "_____ engineers in the world."
A best

True or false The biggest lesson from this section of the chapter is probably that getting qualified recruits to come to you is better than going out and finding them.
A True

"Gamifying the Career Path: L'Oréal's *Reveal* Game"

True or false Job fairs are an effective way to cut through the noise when looking for job recruits.
A False

Q Who was L'Oréal interested in recruiting?
A Qualified job candidates/people with a skill set that weren't on the radar of a high-end makeup brand

Q *Reveal* was a game designed to simulate what kind of experience for players?
A An actual working experience

Q How many people had already signed up to play when *Reveal* officially launched?
A More than 21,000

"Brandstorm: Innovating Recruitment with Real-World Games"

Q In 2012 *Brandstorm* focused on new products for what company?
A The Body Shop

True or false *Brandstorm* recently gave L'Oréal not just the opportunity to find out what kids today will buy but also how they will buy it.
A True

Q How many countries were represented by teams in the 2012 *Brandstorm* competition?
A 40

Q Of particular interest to L'Oréal are potential recruits with a _____ instinct.
A competitive

CHAPTER 9

Solve the Sentence Anagram

Q What industry's gamified programs repeatedly yield the least fun and offer no value and meager rewards—yet are ripe with fresh opportunities for all three?
A Supermarkets with loyalty programs inflate costs and don't offer challenges, rewards, or fun.

INDEX

About the Authors

—

GABE ZICHERMANN is considered the world's foremost expert on designing engagement strategies for customers and employees. As founder and CEO of Gamification Co and chair of the GSummit, he helps catalyze a worldwide community devoted to engagement science and meaningful experience design. Zichermann is also cofounder of Dopamine, the specialist gamification design consultancy, where he works with start-ups, Fortune 500s, and governments to help make the world a more engaging place. Originally from Toronto, Zichermann now lives in New York City where he is codirector of the Founder Institute's NYC chapter and a board governor for StartOut.org. His other passions include public speaking and cooking—and you can experience both vicariously by connecting with him on Facebook and Twitter.

JOSELIN LINDER is an author and former small-business owner. She coauthored *Game-Based Marketing* with Gabe Zichermann in 2010. She has contributed to NPR's *This American Life* and *Morning Edition* as well as served as an author-for-hire on relationship, humor, and game books. Her work has appeared in regular columns for AOL and the blog at gamification.co. Linder lives in Brooklyn, New York, with her husband and their dogs.